Home Town

TALES

Home Town
TALES

Philip Gulley

MULTNOMAH PUBLISHERS
Sisters, Oregon

HOME TOWN TALES
published by Multnomah Publishers, Inc.

© 1998 by Philip Gulley

International Standard Book Number: 1-57673-276-2

Cover photograph by David Bailey

Printed in the United States of America

Unless otherwise indicated, scripture quotations are from *The Holy Bible*, New International Version © 1973, 1984 by International Bible Society, used by permission of Zondervan Publishing House.

For information:
Multnomah Publishers, Inc.•Post Office Box 1720•Sisters, Oregon 97759

Library of Congress Cataloging-in Publication Data
Gulley, Philip.
   Home town tales/by Philip Gulley.
      p. cm.
   ISBN 1-57673-276-2 (paper)
      1. Christian life—Anecdotes. 2. Gulley, Philip. 3. Christian life—
   Quaker authors. I. Title.
BV4517.G86   1998
242—dc21   97–44685
                                                                  CIP

98 99 00 01 02 03 04 05 — 10 9 8 7 6 5 4 3 2 1

CONTENTS

Introduction 8
Preface: A Yardstick of the Soul 10

LOVE
    Ray 17
    The Clothesline 21
    Stitches in Time 25
    Cyrus and Doral 29
    Tender Integrity 33

JOY
    Cat-Feet Quiet 39
    Vesper Magic 42
    Nativity 46
    The Joy of Usefulness 50
    Going Home 54

PEACE
    My Lawn Mower, My Friend 61
    Bedtime Stories 66
    Clyde 70
    Bath People 74
    History Lessons 78

PATIENCE
    Sally and the Pythagorean Theorem . 85
    Margaret and Her Pennies 89
    Our Resident Noah 92
    Town Mottoes 96

PATIENCE, PATIENCE,
PATIENCE!!! *100*

KINDNESS
Warts and All *107*
Kindness Bestowed *111*
Sister Rosalie *115*
Consider the Birds *119*
The Day I Met Paul Harvey *122*

GOODNESS
The Crime Wave *129*
Bernice *133*
Annice *137*
A Tribute to Ned Ludd *142*
The Information Line *145*

FAITHFULNESS
The Unclouded Day *151*
Inheritance Day *155*
The Heist *158*
The Open Door *162*
Dreamers All *165*

GENTLENESS
Fussing, Fighting, and Forgiving . . . *173*
The Admonition Suit *178*
Dump Boy *182*
Rivers of Mercy *186*
Pam *192*

SELF-CONTROL

Getting Rid of Things *199*
State Fair *203*
The Birdhouse *207*
Flowers and Weeds *212*
Leverne *216*

THINGS YOU OUGHT TO KNOW

I am a storyteller, not a historian. History is about facts; stories are about truth. It's important to know the difference. If I were a historian, every memory in this book would be precisely factual. Since I'm a storyteller, I don't have to labor under that burden. Regrettably, we live in an age in which storytellers are suspect. Our search for truth has turned us into Pharisees who strain at gnats and swallow camels. I think truth comes robed in all sorts of garments.

The stories in this book are true, if by "true" you mean "honest to the human condition." If by "true" you mean "cold, hard fact," then this book is not always true. I can't always recall exactly what folks said, though the values they conveyed return to me crystal clear. I've changed some names, uprooted some folks and replanted them in my hometown, and once or twice made my life seem a little more interesting than it really is. Please forgive me, but that's the kind of thing we storytellers do.

I dedicate this book to Tom Mullen, John Van Diest, Don Jacobson, Dina Kinnan, and the Paul Harveys, both Jr. and Sr., who saw promise in my writing and did something about it.

I dedicate it to Joan, Spencer, and Sam, who fill our home with love.

I dedicate it to Mom and Dad and Chick, Glenn,

Doug, and David, who've forgiven me for writing about them.

I dedicate it to the people of my hometown—Danville, Indiana. They are forever on my mind and in my heart.

I dedicate it to my coministers—the kind people of Irvington Friends Meeting and the good folks at Multnomah Publishers, all of whom make me appear more competent than I am.

Finally, I dedicate this book to our friend and guide, Jesus Christ, who, when he wasn't riding the Pharisees, told some pretty fine stories himself.

A YARDSTICK OF THE SOUL

In the summer of my twelfth year, a new family moved into our neighborhood. They were from Chicago, which made them a novelty in my town. Had they been Unitarians, it wouldn't have caused the stir being from Chicago did. To return to school the day after Labor Day and write in your what-I-did-on-my-summer-vacation essay that you had visited Chicago automatically propelled you into the ranks of the worldly. Smoking cigarettes on the playground paled by comparison.

They moved into the old Sweeney house—which we thought beyond redemption—thereby confirming our suspicions that people from the city, while sophisticated in some ways, were in other ways woefully unenlightened. The Sweeney house, to put it kindly, was the quintessential "before" picture. Its chief role was to make the rest of us content with our lot, and it served that purpose wonderfully. A man down on his luck could wander by the Sweeney house and come away feeling blessed beyond measure.

The only thing the Sweeney house had going for it was a strong foundation, which is not to be discounted, though in this case it was not enough. After all, what rests on a foundation is every bit as critical as the base itself. What rested on the Sweeney foundation were boards spongy-soft with rot. It was like pulling on five-dollar pants over hundred-dollar shoes.

What the Chicago family had hoped for was mere cosmetic change, a facelift for an old and sagging lady, but it was not to be. Halfway into the summer they realized that surgery of a more invasive nature was needed. I remember that day well. It was the Fourth of July neighborhood cookout. The men collected around the grill, talking home maintenance, while we boys listened from the fringes. The Chicago man said he was going to start over at the foundation. The other men nodded their sympathy, though I sensed in them a smug pleasure that their assessment of the Sweeney home had been confirmed.

Tearing a house down is infinitely sadder than building it. When the house my wife and I lived in during the first years of our marriage was torn down, we stood outside watching. The pain was surprising in its severity. We had hoped someday to drive the children by and point out where Mommy and Daddy had lived years before, where the star from our first Christmas tree had scratched the ceiling, where we had refinished the rocking chair we'd used to lull them to sleep. Now there was nothing to show.

The day the Sweeney house came down, we gathered to observe. Even the Sweeneys came by. The demise of this neighborhood eyesore was so pleasant for us that we scarcely noticed the grim set to their faces. Twenty-five years later I remember it and wonder what memories that house held for them. What is junk to one is priceless to another.

Still, even in dying, a hint of promise can be found—a

sensing that death, in its cold way, is simply a stepping aside so new life might have its turn. In this manner new life came to the Sweeney house as fresh, white lumber rose up from the hundred-year-old foundation. I watched it ascend board by clean board. The man from Chicago would stop every couple of hours to drink a Coke, and we would talk of carpentry—mostly about framing a house and how it was imperative that everything be plumb-straight lest wind and time reduce the house to rubble.

I drive by that house today and admire its clean lines. Though it is not an altogether attractive house, it is strong and crisp and thus has my respect. It reminds me that we are not called to be pretty, but to be fruitful and faithful and true. Besides, time has a way of conferring beauty, which is why a simple Shaker meetinghouse still moves us after two hundred years.

As with houses, some lives are more true and commendable than others. We have an odd way of showing this in our culture—showering athletes with acclaim and fortune while paying social workers a relatively meager subsistence. What is needed is a unit of measure which more accurately reflects one's constitution and contribution—a yardstick of the soul, so to speak. In the fruit of the Spirit such a yardstick is found.

On the wall of my workshop, my children's growth is carefully recorded. Once a year they stand in stocking feet, a line is drawn on the wall marking their height, and the date is recorded. (Whenever I get a job offer, I ask myself if the new job merits leaving that wall behind.) My parents have a similar wall in their home. A look at it indicates that my height leveled out years ago. Now another way to measure my development has taken its place—my growth in love, joy, peace, patience, kindness, goodness, faithfulness, gentleness, and self-control (Galatians 5:22–23). Some days I measure up; some days I don't. Still, stretching ourselves against this wall of spiritual fruit and taking our measure is an important exercise and one we ought to continue.

The purpose of such a measuring is not to provoke guilt, but rather to remind us of those treasures which never lose their value.

While you read this book, I ask you to remember that a once-beautiful home was laid waste by neglect and inattention and that a man from Chicago labored to make it useful and true once more. And I ask you to celebrate the Christ who can cause the most barren life to yield sweet fruit. I pray such a life for you.

The fruit of the Spirit

is love . . .

Ray

I met Ray the first year I moved to the city. He worships at a Quaker meeting near his hometown of Dublin except when the roads are icy; then he worships at our meeting-house. His Quaker meeting doesn't have a pastor. They sit in silence and wait for the Lord to give them a message, as the old Quakers used to do.

Ray is suspicious of pastors and said so within five minutes of meeting me. "Most pastors like nothing more than to bully people," he told me. I replied that we pastors take classes in seminary on how to bully people.

Then he told me he didn't believe Jesus is God.

That's when I made up my mind I wasn't going to spend a lot of time with Ray. The next morning the phone rang, early. It was Ray.

"I'd like to take you to breakfast," he said. "I want to talk with you. Most pastors I've met don't know their theology. I want to see if you're any different." It wasn't a request; it was an order, a command appearance.

Ray drove by and picked me up. We went to Bob Evans and ordered pancakes. He asked me what I thought of the Trinity. I told him I believed in it. He disagreed. I started to worry. Ray was nearly eighty years old then, but vigorous. If push came to shove, I think he could have taken me. But Ray is a pacifist; he disagreed with me, then paid for my pancakes.

A month later it snowed again. Ray showed up at our meetinghouse. We sang "Are You Washed in the Blood?" It's a rollicking old revival tune. We sing it whenever our worship needs livening up.

Ray took me to breakfast at Bob Evans the next morning.

"I don't like blood songs," he told me. "That's beastly theology."

Now when it snows on Sunday, I make sure we sing "Are You Washed in the Blood?" Ray sits in the front row and grits his teeth.

Ray doesn't attend our Quaker meeting in the summer because the road to his meetinghouse is wide open. But once a month, generally on Sunday evenings, the phone rings. It'll be Ray.

"Let's go for a root beer," he'll say. "My treat."

I drive by and pick him up. We motor over to Edward's Drive-In where they serve root beer in a frosty mug. We sit in the car, sip root beer, and discuss German theologians of the 1930s. I point out to Ray how all of them believed Jesus is divine. Ray thinks about that for a while, then says, "Well, don't forget, those same folks voted for Hitler." Ray has an answer for everything.

Initially, I hadn't intended to befriend Ray. I'm just orthodox enough to believe God might zap a man who denies the deity of Jesus as boldly as Ray does. But we have to get our thrills somewhere. Some men have a weakness for fast women. I have a soft spot for eighty-year-old heretics who buy me pancakes and root beer.

Before Ray became a Quaker, he went away to World War II. His pastor saw him off to war by telling him to kill as many soldiers as he could. I think that's when Ray started having trouble with pastors. When he came home, he took up with the Quakers. He met his wife, Marjorie. They had three children. The kids grew up and moved away, and Marjorie was diagnosed with Alzheimer's. When Ray had to put her in a nursing home, he sat by her bedside holding her hand long after she'd forgotten who he was.

A few days after Marjorie died, Ray came by our house. He sat in the rocking chair holding our baby, Sam. Sam came into this world about the same time Ray's wife left it. I think in Ray's mind, baby Sam is a replacement. Ray calls him "my dear, little Sam." He rocks Sam back and forth, his eyes cloudy with tears. He tells me I'm a blessed man. On this we agree.

Ray still doesn't believe Jesus is God. And he still doesn't like blood songs. If orthodoxy were a requirement for friendship with me, Ray and I would be enemies. But it isn't, so Ray and I are friends. Besides, I've always thought that what is in a man's heart is even more important than what is in his head. I got that idea from the apostle Paul, who once wrote that love is the greatest gift of all.

The
Clothesline

everal years ago, Dan and Joy, a Mennonite couple, moved into our neighborhood next door to Ray Stewart. Ray is a Quaker, and though he doesn't attend the meeting I pastor, he is quick to inform me of potential converts.

"Had some Mennonites move in next door. You ought to go see them before the Disciples preacher gets wind of them," Ray told me.

Later that week when I was out for a walk, I stopped to welcome them to the neighborhood. They'd moved into the old Crewes home. Joan and I had thought about buying that house ourselves and had gone to look at it when it was up for sale. But when we saw water stains on the parlor ceiling, our enthusiasm for home ownership dimmed.

When I stopped to visit, Dan was in the parlor peering at the ceiling, an anxious look on his face. I was grateful the ceiling was his problem and not mine. We exchanged introductions, and I invited

Dan and Joy to our meeting for worship. With that innocent invitation, the course of my life was forever changed.

It began with their brick driveway. When the Crewes built the house back in the 1930s, they didn't put in a driveway. Dan dug down eight inches and put in a brick sidewalk and a place to park their cars. They used the dug-up dirt to make raised flower beds along the edge of their property. My wife, Joan, stopped in for a visit. Joy showed her the new flower beds. This was when Joan started talking about our making raised flower beds. I asked her where we would get the dirt. "We can use the dirt you'll dig up making our new brick sidewalk," she said.

A few weeks later, Joy and Joan were talking after worship. Joan commented on Joy's clothesline. Joy comes from Amish people and hasn't yet made her peace with machines that blow hot, stale air on your clothes. They strung up a clothesline from the edge of their back porch over to their garage. It is the only clothesline in our neighborhood. When Sam, our two-year-old, saw their sheets fluttering in the breeze, he clapped his hands and yelled, "Circus, circus!"

Joy was telling Joan how nice it is to fall asleep on sun-dried sheets. Joan remembered that smell from her childhood and the next day commented that she would like a clothesline. "Plus, think of the money we'll save on electricity," she told me. It was my day off, so I went to the lumberyard and bought the wood. Then I went to the hardware store to buy the line, eye bolts, and cement to set the posts. It cost seventy dollars in all. Saving money, I was learning, could be quite expensive.

Though Dan and Joy only have a one-wire clothesline, ours has three wires. I take a strange delight in besting a Mennonite. The posts are set twenty-five feet apart. We can hang the entire week's wash at one time. Sam and Spencer play among the sheets. Next spring, we're going to plant morning glories at the base of the poles and train them along the lines. We'll lose drying space, but the extra beauty will be worth it. I'm hoping it'll take Joan's mind off the brick sidewalk and raised flower beds.

People from our church come by to visit, and we sit outside underneath the shade trees while our family underwear flaps on the line. My slender sons have tiny Mickey Mouse and Tigger underwear. In comparison, my underwear are large and ratty. They beat the air like flags. My fellow Quakers steal glances at them and shudder. It's hampered my ministry with them. I stand in the pulpit and preach about such lofty, wondrous things as salvation by grace, and they ignore me. They've seen my underwear. Now I'm just another bozo with holes in his skivvies. I'm probably going to have to leave this church and start over somewhere else.

Truthfully, I'm thinking our clothesline will be a blessing. People have a tendency to revere their pastor. I don't think that's always good. It obscures our humanity. You need to see our undies flapping on the line to remember that we are human.

Do we love people for who they are? Or do we love them for who we think they ought to be? I sit underneath those shade trees and visit with couples who've been married more years than I've been alive. Folks who love each other for who they are, not for who they ought to be. A big problem in our world is that we fall in love with images instead of persons. God forbid that our underwear should show, that our masks should slip.

These Mennonites moved into our staid, proper neighborhood and hung out their skivvies for all to see. That's who we are, they told us. No pretensions. Their arrival was providential, God-directed. We were growing snobby. A friend of mine lives in a subdivision where clotheslines are a violation of covenant rules. They don't want to see your underwear and don't want you to see theirs. Repression and image are the neighborhood bywords. That was where we were headed.

Love, the Bible teaches, does not put on airs. It took a few Mennonites moving into the old Crewes place to remind us of that ancient truth.

Stitches
in Time

*E*lectricity was discovered by the ancient Greeks, though it didn't find its way to my in-laws' farm until the summer of 1948. That's when the truck from the Orange County Rural Electric Cooperative made its way down Grimes Lake Road, planting poles and stringing wire. My mother-in-law, Ruby, sat on her front porch snapping beans while the linemen set the poles. That night she asked her husband, Howard, what he thought of her getting an electric sewing machine. Her treadle sewing machine was broken, the victim of two high-spirited boys who had pumped the treadle to an early death.

They drove to Bedford the next day to the Singer Sewing Center and bought a brand-new electric Singer with a buttonholer, a cabinet, and a chair. It cost two hundred and forty dollars, money they'd earned from selling a truckload of hogs to the meatpacking plant in New Solsberry.

Ruby set into sewing for her boys. They added three children to their flock. More sewing. After supper, when the table was cleared and dishes washed, Ruby would bend over the machine, churning out clothes for her children and her neighbors. Thousands of dresses and shirts and pants. Clothes for dolls. Clothes for the minister's wife in town. Prom dresses. Wedding dresses. The Singer raised its needle millions of times. Her family would fall asleep under Ruby-made quilts, lulled to sleep by the Singer hum.

The kids grew up and moved away. Grandchildren came, eight in all. The Singer stitched maternity clothes, baby dresses, baptismal gowns, and quilts for the cribs. In 1987, Ruby called us on the phone, discouraged. After thirty-nine years, her Singer was limping. She took it to Mr. Gardner in the next town over. He fixed sewing machines but couldn't revive hers. He sent it away to Chicago. A month later it came back, a paper tag hanging from its cord. *Obsolete. Parts not available*, the tag read.

I went to a sewing machine store the next day to buy a new one. Her old one was metal. The new machines are plastic and have computers and cost the same as Ruby's first car. They give classes on how to use them. In the display window was a 1948 metal Singer blackhead.

"Does that one work?" I asked the man.

"I don't know," he said. "Let's plug it in." He plugged it in. It hummed to life.

"It's not for sale," he told me. "It's a display. There aren't a lot of these old Singer blackheads around anymore."

I told him about Ruby—how she lives by herself and sews to keep busy, how she only charges six dollars to make a dress because the people she sews for don't have a lot of money, how a lot of times she doesn't charge a dime, how sewing is her ministry.

He sold the machine to me for twenty-five dollars.

The next weekend we hauled it down to Ruby's. She was sitting on the front porch, watching for our car to round the corner on the gravel lane. She came outside and stood by the car as we opened the trunk. As she peered down at the '48 blackhead, a smile creased her face.

"It's just like my old one," she whispered.

We wrestled it inside and installed it in her old cabinet. Perfect fit. Plugged it in. When Ruby heard the hum, she clapped her hands.

It's still going strong. Ruby still charges six dollars a dress—unless it's a bride's dress; then she sews it by hand. That'll cost you fifteen dollars, but only if you can afford it.

Ruby travels north to visit her granddaughter Rachael. Rachael shows Ruby her Barbie doll, then asks Ruby if she could maybe please sew some clothes for Barbie. The first night Ruby is home, she bends over her '48 blackhead, stitching matching dresses for Rachael and her Barbie. Way past midnight she sews. The next morning she drives to town and mails a package northward. Three days later the phone rings. It's Rachael calling to say "Thank you" and "I love you" and "When can I see you again?"

On two other occasions, my wife and I found 1948 Singer blackheads in antique stores. We bought them and gave them to Ruby. She's got a lot of sewing ahead, and we don't want her to run out of sewing machines before she runs out of things to sew.

I don't always applaud every new thing that comes down the road, though I'm grateful that in 1948 electricity made its way down the Grimes Lake Road. I'm grateful, too, for a woman who sews way into the night, who dispenses love one stitch at a time.

Cyrus
and Doral

When I was growing up, we had our hometown newspaper to keep us apprised of news large and small. Owning a small-town newspaper requires a deft touch. If you report everything that happens, people won't talk with you. You have to be mindful of reputations. It's perfectly proper to report that Rebecca Lawson won first place in the Optimist Club speech contest. But in the "Courtroom News" section, you forego full names and use initials. It's a lot less interesting, but it makes for a peaceful community. Denial does a thriving business in most small towns.

If you wanted the real news in our town, you had to visit the card rack at the Rexall. It was the only card rack in town, so anyone wanting to placate or woo someone with a card would inevitably end up at Rexall poring over the meager offering of poetry and prose under the watchful gaze of Thad Cramer, the town's pharmacist. An observant citizen could learn a great deal by watching the cards people bought.

I was there one morning when Howard Barry walked in. He began reading cards in the "I'm sorry" section. During the next six months, I kept an ear turned toward the Barry drama. Sure enough, Howard and Betty divorced. *H.B. and B.B.: dissolution of marital vows*, it read in the "Courtroom News" section of the newspaper. Everyone else was caught unaware, but I had known all along something was amiss. Men like Howard Barry don't buy "I'm sorry" cards unless things have gone desperately wrong.

The card rack was also a good place to find out what was happening on the budding-romance front.

Cyrus and his wife, Earlene, lived down the street from us and would pass summer evenings on their porch swing. Cyrus was retired from the General Motors factory in the city, and Earlene worked part-time at the school as a cook. Two kids, both married. No grandchildren yet, but dropping hints and hoping. Then Earlene came down with cancer, left home for the hospital and never came back. Cyrus took to sitting inside, watching TV and eating TV dinners. After a while he even gave up his seat at church. When you've been sharing a pew with your beloved for thirty-five years, sitting in church by yourself on Sunday morning holds a pain we can scarcely imagine.

After a few months, Cyrus's daughter waded in and took charge. She drove him to the doctor for a checkup and signed him up for Meals on Wheels. The next Monday a volunteer stopped by his house with a hot meal and a warm smile. Doral was her name. Sixty-two years old, big heart with energy to burn. Cyrus came to the door in a T-shirt and house slippers. Doral carried the meal inside, sat Cyrus down at the table, laid out the silverware, handed him a napkin, and patted his sad shoulder.

"There, there," she told him, "it gets a little easier every day." Doral was the voice of experience, having lost her husband two years earlier.

By the next summer, Cyrus was answering the door in a new shirt, and Doral was staying through dessert.

I found all of this out from Cyrus himself, down at the Rexall. I was there buying a card for my girlfriend when Cyrus came over to survey the "I love you" cards. We stood shoulder to shoulder, sixteen and sixty, searching for the just-right card to convey our affections.

He wished me well.

"I was your age when I met my dear Earlene," he confided. "Thirty-five years of marriage we had together."

I told my girlfriend about Cyrus. Her family used

to sit right behind Cyrus and Earlene at church.

"Cyrus is back," she told me. "Sitting in a different pew. And the nicest woman comes with him."

Cyrus and Doral were married twelve years; then Cyrus died in his sleep. Doral still delivers Meals on Wheels, while Cyrus rests at the South Cemetery next to his beloved Earlene. That was Doral's idea.

Oddly enough, it was a bachelor named Paul who wrote the truest words about love. "Love is not jealous… it does not insist on its own way." The minister intoned those very words at Cyrus and Doral's wedding. It appears to me Doral took them to heart.

Tender
Integrity

I have a friend named Tom who pastors a church over in Ohio. We used to pastor in the same town, but that was three churches ago for Tom. Every so often we visit on the phone. He tells me his latest thoughts on church growth. Tom has a lot of ideas concerning church growth, none of which seem to take hold. This past year, he was betting on mimes to pack in the crowds.

The idea came to him during worship. "If you have mimes, they will come!" a voice whispered. So at the next meeting of elders, he talked about bringing gospel truth and revival through the ministry of miming. These elders are nice people, which is how they got to be elders. They believe in niceness, even at the expense of truth.

"Now there's a good idea, Pastor," they told him. "Why don't you organize a special Sunday evening service with mimes? That's a fine idea. We'll look forward to that. Mimes—why didn't we think of that?"

Tom found two mimes, set up the worship service, ran ads in the paper, brought in extra chairs, showed up early to unlock the doors, and waited for the crowds. But no one came except the mimes and Bill, the janitor. Everyone else stayed home and watched *60 Minutes*. They were just being nice and didn't have the courage to tell him the truth—that a worship service with mimes was the dumbest idea they'd ever heard and they wouldn't attend if their lives depended on it.

Tom was furious. He called me on the phone. "I am so tired of nice people who lie to keep from hurting my feelings," he said.

As a result, Tom has committed himself to telling the truth. He tells people what he thinks, whether they want to know or not. Like the lady who's done his church's newsletter for the past twenty years, the worst church newsletter in the kingdom of God. Tom told her he thought the newsletter needed freshening up and that she should take out the column that lists all the people who missed a Sunday. So she took it out, and now she's writing a column rating his sermons. One Bible means the sermon was bad; four Bibles means the sermon was good. According to her, Tom's been giving a lot of one-Bible sermons lately.

But he is happier than I've ever seen him. "For the very first time, I can look that woman in the eye, and she can look me right back. No more hiding behind polite little lies. I think we might even end up loving each other," he told me.

I've been thinking on this—how when truth is lacking, love cannot be found. But when folks value truth over niceness, love has a chance to take root. John Woolman was an honest Quaker from way back. He got away with it because he combined truth-telling with tenderness, something I often forget to do. Tender integrity. He once wrote, "To see the failings of our friends and think hard of them, without opening that which we ought to open, and still carry a face of friendship—this tends to undermine the foundation of true unity."

Truth is the highest expression of love. A lot of times I won't say something to folks because I don't want to hurt them and I want to be liked. Whenever I do that, I try to convince myself that I'm practicing love. But I delude myself. Love looks you straight in the eye and speaks truth. When we fail to do that, it's generally because we value personal comfort more than another's growth. Love takes a person by the hand and speaks truth and leaves that person better. Tender integrity.

Here's a good test to know whether or not truth-telling springs from love. Truth will not only pain those who hear it; it will pain those who speak it. If we don't love someone, it won't hurt at all to speak truth. We'll tell them what we think with no regard for their feelings. If telling the truth is fun, it probably doesn't come from love. Jeremiah told the truth and was called the "weeping prophet."

Sometimes truth brings tears. This is why some folks, despite being good people, will settle for niceness over truth. A poor trade. I think of love and truth as twins forever joined. When one goes a certain way, the other is bound to follow.

The fruit of the Spirit

is love, joy . . .

Cat-Feet
Quiet

Of all the things I miss from my youth, heading the list would be soda pop. Soda pop was at its best when it came in glass bottles plucked from the ice-water chest at Logan's Mobil. Plus, if you gave Logan's your soda business, Wally and Bill would patch your bike tires for free.

Wally and Bill were the owners of Logan's, having bought the business from Pop Logan. They never changed the name, knowing folks would call it Logan's no matter what they named it. People in my hometown don't take to change. My parents have lived in their house for more than twenty-seven years, but it's still called the old Hollowell place after the people who lived there fifty years before.

So Wally and Bill retained the name and the soda pop cooler, which was up front by the cash register and the Juicy Fruit rack. Soda cost a dime. If you were in a hurry and wanted to take the bottle with you, it cost twelve cents. They would waive the extra two cents if you promised to bring the bottle back. But we were seldom in a hurry, so we would drink the soda while sitting on the cooler—the closest thing we had to air conditioning.

If humanity has devised a more pleasant way to pass a hot August afternoon, that way has escaped me. Pedaling your Schwinn Typhoon to Logan's after a game of baseball, your throat scratchy with thirst. Opening the cooler and surveying the rainbow of flavors—Nehi Grape, Choc-ola, Mason's Root Beer, Double Cola, Royal Crown, Orange Crush, and Big Chief. Plunging your arm deep into the icy water and pulling out heaven. Sliding your dime across the glass-topped counter. Wally asking, "Drinking it here or taking it with you?"

"Here," you'd answer, arranging yourself on the cooler, then drinking deep. If you were quiet enough, Oscar, the gas station cat, might settle in your lap. Nirvana. The quality of any given place increases exponentially if there's a good cat in the picture. You should be so lucky to have a cat take a liking to you. Oscar made a good place even better.

A couple of years back, I heard of a gas station that still sold soda in bottles from an ice-water cooler. It was in a little town an hour and a half from my home, which seemed a paltry distance to drive for such a treasure. On my next day off, I went. Prices had changed—from ten cents to fifty. Sixty cents if you're in a hurry and take the bottle with you. I stayed. Sat on the cooler, Coke in one hand, peanuts in the other. But the joy wasn't there.

Joy, after all, isn't something one orders up. It sneaks in on cat's feet and snuggles in your lap though you didn't call its name. You look down and there it is—come to pay you a visit.

There's a story in the Bible about two disciples trudging down Emmaus Road after Jesus was killed. They were joined by a stranger who walked with them until suppertime. "Eat with us," they invited, "we have plenty." Those were lean years, and a free supper was nothing to sneeze at. So he lingered, gave thanks for the bread, and passed it around. Those disciples had no more than taken a bite when they recognized that stranger as Jesus. After a collective "Wow!" they hustled back to Jerusalem to share the Resurrection news.

Joy visits when we least expect it—we're ten years old and drinking deep from heaven's bottle, or life has bottomed out and Jesus drops in. Cat-feet quiet. It isn't that God withholds it; joy is always looking to climb into our laps. It's just that joy needs silence and thus seldom settles into the lap of a noisy person. It's only when we stop talking long enough to whisper grace that joy has a way of rubbing against us, curling in our lap, making its presence known.

Vesper
Magic

My hometown is the county seat of Hendricks County, which gives us what no other town in our county has—a courthouse lawn. We used to rub it in by holding summer concerts there, something no other town in our county could do. Though our fellow countians coveted our setting, they never envied our music, most of which was provided by townspeople whose most commendable feature was that they would play for free. This means we heard a lot of bad country-and-western music, except when some teenagers played—then we heard a lot of bad rock and roll. It was painful to listen to, but then being part of a community isn't always sweetness and light.

In the mid-'80s, the town board moved the concerts down to Ellis Park and brought in the Indianapolis Symphony Orchestra. They never told us what prompted such a radical departure from tradition, though it likely had something to do with trying to redeem our town's taste in music which had been heading south at a steady clip. Too much "Achy Breaky Heart," not enough Vivaldi.

They charged six dollars a head, which caused a stir. When you've been getting free music for twenty years and suddenly have to pay for it, someone's bound to fuss. But everyone showed up anyway, since in my town not showing up means getting talked about. The highlight of the evening was when the symphony played Sousa's "Stars and Stripes Forever." Ray Whitaker and Jerry Weed shot off fireworks from Turner's cornfield next to the park. Ray works for the town, and Jerry owns the fabric shop. They stuck the Roman candles in a plastic tube, lit the fuses, and ran for the woods. Now we hire some outfit from out of town that uses computers and timed fuses and blasts off the fireworks in time with Sousa. It costs a lot more money, but it seemed the wiser course after Ray almost took a bottle rocket in the hindquarters one year. Ray's the only one who knows how to run the town waterworks, and we want to keep him healthy.

Every year Joan and I take our lawn chairs and head to the park for a listen. Things get a little fancier all the time. The orchestra began by playing on a mowed-off corner of the Babe Ruth outfield; now it plays under a fabric dome and spotlights. Pap Martin wrote out a check for the dome. (He doesn't want anyone to know, so you need to keep that a secret.)

One year, the orchestra played Broadway show tunes. An out-of-state baritone flew in and sang "The Impossible Dream," which is about as good as music gets. Sitting under moonlight listening to *Man of La Mancha* and thinking that anything's possible—a cure for cancer, falling in love, maybe even Jesus coming on the clouds in glory. What is it about music that excites our imaginations and brings such joy?

When I worked my way through college at a nursing home, a singing preacher would come in every Sunday afternoon and lead a hymn sing—"Amazing Grace," "Shall We Gather at the River," and "We'll Understand It Better." Folks would drag themselves down to sing, then two-step back. Oh, how light our steps become when music is in our hearts!

The early Quakers didn't believe in music. They thought it was frivolous and tended to take their minds off weightier matters. After a couple hundred years they lightened up, and now we give the Methodists a run for their money. It's a poor religion that isn't able to make room for joy. I'm glad we Quakers had a change of heart.

It is no accident that the Bible resonates with music—from David strumming his lyre to Paul and Silas belting out hymns in jail. The Bible doesn't say what Paul and Silas sang, only that when they did, the walls shook and the doors swung open. Music has the power to break down many a barrier. King David even danced naked in the streets of Jerusalem when the victory music got fast and furious. While this is not advisable today, it's good to know there's a biblical precedent just in case we are ever similarly tempted.

I consider these some of the most joyful moments of my life: the day I said "I do," those days my sons were born, and sitting in a lawn chair at Ellis Park while the orchestra performed its vesper magic and Ray and Jerry aimed for the stars.

Nativity

My mother-in-law, Ruby, lives in southern Indiana in the town of Paoli. We spend family Christmas with her. Those good people in Paoli remember what Christmas is all about. Each year, just before Thanksgiving, Herb from the street department hauls the baby Jesus, his mommy and daddy, and an assortment of livestock and shepherds and wise men out of storage and sets them up on the courthouse lawn. The holy family takes up residence on the southwest corner of the square, and no one dares to complain. There are no civil libertarians in Paoli at Christmastime.

But Christmas isn't official until Wilson Roberts decorates his variety store, which he does the day after Thanksgiving. Each year the same adornments—a cardboard cutout of Rudolph taped to the front window, a strand of tinsel hung over the checkout counter, and a bucket of candy canes left over from the year before sitting next to the cash register. On that day, at precisely 8:50

A.M., people from all over town head to the variety store to start their gift buying. It is a migration every bit as predictable as the Capistrano swallows.

I stopped in a few years ago, looking for a nativity set. The week before, my wife had said, "What this house needs is a nativity set." So on the day after Thanksgiving, while everyone else was lying around in a turkey-filled stupor, I drove into town to the variety store. It's a small store in sore need of a liquidation sale. Wilson's motto is "We have it, if we can find it." Forty years of merchandise is stacked to the ceiling. It makes for some incongruent discoveries. I once found a poster of Michael Jackson next to a 1959 edition of *The Old Farmer's Almanac*.

I went inside and sought out Wilson Roberts. He was sitting in the back of the store, smoking a cigar, his ashes dribbling on the wood floor.

"I'd like to buy a nativity set," I told him.

He said, "Well, I know we have one, if I can just find it."

He began to look. He looked over by the hair nets and bobby pins. Not there. He looked by the garden hoses. Not there. Then over by the yard goods and notions. No holy family there, either. He looked over near the lawn chairs, then underneath the candy display, which is where he found it.

He dusted off the box, opened it, and took a roll

call. One manger, one kneeling mother, one proud father, some shepherds, three wise men, one sheep, one cow, one donkey, and one baby Jesus. Everyone present and accounted for.

"That'll be twelve dollars," he told me.

"How about ten?" I countered. The box was torn, and the cow was missing an ear.

Wilson Roberts squinted at me, shifted his cigar from one side of his mouth to the other, then said, "You got a deal." So now we have a nativity set. French-made. *Genuine plaster from Paris*, the box says.

The day I bought the nativity set was the last time I saw Wilson Roberts alive. He died the next year. We drive past his old store on our way to Thanksgiving dinner at Ruby's. The variety store is closed now. When he died, it died. Then Wal-Mart moved in, and people talk as if it's a blessing. I guarantee you Wal-Mart won't have a 1959 edition of *The Old Farmer's Almanac*. Don't even bother to ask.

I think back on Wilson Roberts searching amid bobby pins and yard goods for the baby Jesus. Sometimes our search for the Divine has us poking around in all kinds of corners.

Every year at Christmas, I haul our nativity set out of storage and place it on the piano next to our front door. That way, when we're scurrying about in a frenzy, honoring the birth of the One who told us not to be anxious about anything, we can pause and remember what Christmas is all about. How that quiet baby came into this tumultuous world, greeted by wide-eyed shepherds and one-eared cows. I swing open my heart and welcome him home.

The Joy of Usefulness

I became a pastor because I wanted to help people. Why the yearning to help others led to the pastoral ministry and not, say, to a career in medicine is a mystery I've yet to decipher. It's all the better if you can follow your joy and drive a nice car, too. Still, I'm not complaining. I like being a pastor, especially on those rare occasions when I've helped someone along life's way.

I call them rare occasions because the people in my Quaker meeting haven't asked me for much help lately. They're an amazingly self-sufficient group of people who bear life's burdens with silent equanimity. In addition to their stoic nature, they are incredibly robust. Thus, I am seldom called to help them.

Two of my best friends, Stan and Jim, are also pastors. They spend their days traveling from hospital to hospital, comforting one troubled soul after another. At night they collapse in their beds, content with the memory of a useful day. I linger near the phone, praying for a call to take me from my warm home to the bedside of a wretched parishioner. The call seldom comes.

Is it too much for me to expect my people to have problems? If they've asked me to be their pastor, am I wrong to expect them to have an occasional problem that might occupy my time and help me feel needed?

I don't think this is too much to expect. My friend's congregation was decimated by a pernicious virus. I'm not asking for that. I don't want to be so busy that I'd miss watching *The Andy Griffith Show* every lunch hour. But if a few persons could see their way clear to contracting a mild disease, that would be considerate. It wouldn't have to be anything exotic. Once a lady in my meeting was afflicted with Bell's palsy. It caused her mouth to droop, and she lost all the feeling on one side of her face. Then, after I spent two glorious days by her bedside, her condition grew better and she was completely healed. It was a wonderful illness! She received much-needed bed rest, and I knew the exquisite joy of helpful ministry.

I know I'm not alone in my desire to feel useful. If a woman spends twelve years learning to be a surgeon, I bet she's anxious to perform her first operation. If a man goes away to technical school and studies car repair, he probably can't wait to crawl underneath a chassis. Doesn't a free country owe its citizens the right to ply their chosen trades? Isn't that what America is all about?

Back when I was growing up, our town had a volunteer fire department. They screeched the fire alarm once a week, and all the firefighters practiced rushing to the station. After a while, they grew discouraged because real fires were few and far between. One of our more thoughtful citizens, on a beautiful autumn weekend afternoon, set his field ablaze, thereby earning the gratitude of many of our townspeople. Our policeman got to block the nearby roads. Our firefighters got to fight a real fire. Our newspaper reporter got to write a story. Our insurance agent got to process a claim for damaged crops. And the minister at the Baptist church got to visit the considerate citizen that very evening and profess thanksgiving that no one was hurt. By day's end, everyone felt the pleasant exhaustion of usefulness and went to bed happy. It was one of our town's finer days.

Keith Miller once said, "Jesus never went out of his way to help anybody." The first time I heard that, it angered me. That's an awful thing to say about Jesus. Then I thought about it for a while and understood what Miller was saying. Jesus never went out of his way to help anybody because helping people was never "out of his way." It was the very reason for his existence.

I've told my wife that when I die I want that chiseled on my gravestone: *Here lies Philip Gulley. He never went out of his way to help anybody.* Though, knowing my luck, they'll run out of room and just put *Here lies Philip Gulley. He never helped anybody.* Which might be closer to the truth, unless my church starts cooperating.

Going Home

My parents still live in the house in which I grew up. We visit them once a month, usually on Sundays after church. My sister, her husband, and their three children visit on Sundays too. That's nine extra people, five of whom are under five years old. Before we had children, my parents would invite us to stay for supper. Our visits would linger into the evening. Now they call and say, "Why don't you come visit us this Sunday from three o'clock to four forty-five?"

My wife keeps our television in the closet and frowns when I take it out. My parents indulge themselves with cable television. When we visit in the winter, I go upstairs by myself. I tell them I need a little quiet time with the Lord, but what I do is sit in the easy chair in my brother's old bedroom and channel-surf. Thirty-six channels. One time I caught an *Andy Griffith Show* marathon and watched four straight episodes. It was a glorious Sabbath.

In the summer I drive around town. I like to go back to 29 Martin Drive, where we lived until I was eight years old. The maple trees my dad planted in the side yard now tower over the house. When I lived there they were pencil thin, and we used them for second and third bases. The people who live there now have added a garage. Other than that, things look the same. Once when I passed, the owners were working in the yard. I stopped to visit and dropped hints that I'd like to see the inside of the house, but they didn't invite me in. I remember the exact place I was sitting when my mother taught me to tie my shoes. I'd like to go back in that house and sit at that very place again.

When the house was being built, my dad took some leftover concrete and fashioned a big heart, about a foot across. He took a trowel and etched *Bud and Glo* into the heart. Those are my parents' names—Bud and Glo Gulley. When they moved, they took the heart with them. Today it sits on the ground at the base of their back steps. Someday my parents will die, and we children will divide their belongings. When it comes my turn to pick something, I'm going to choose that concrete heart Dad made for Mom some forty years ago.

I especially liked summers at Martin Drive. We didn't have air conditioning, so in the evenings we'd sit outside on our back porch. If it was near payday, Mom would go to Johnston's IGA and buy the ingredients for homemade ice cream. Dad would sit on the back step and let us take turns cranking the handle on the blue wooden ice-cream maker. After we couldn't turn it anymore, Dad would drape a towel over the maker while the ice cream cured. As an adult I had a hand-cranked ice-cream maker, but I gave it away before our boys came along. I'm in the market for another one. I want my kids to know the feel of turning the crank on an ice-cream maker, how it starts out easy and gets progressively harder. It's a good way to teach them how something worth having takes a little effort.

Twenty-nine Martin Drive had an eat-in kitchen, living room, one bathroom, and three bedrooms. My sister got her own bedroom since she was the only girl. We four boys shared a room until my dad added an extra room. I drive by today and marvel that seven people used to live in that house, though it didn't seem crowded at the time. Houses today are a lot bigger, and kids don't share bedrooms anymore. I'm not sure that's the blessing we make it out to be.

The house my wife and I live in now was built about the same time as 29 Martin Drive. It's a small house, too. Once a year, I think about buying a big, old house with a front porch and fireplace. Joan doesn't understand this.

"Why do we need more room?" she asks me.

"So the kids can have their privacy and we can have ours," I tell her.

She says privacy is overrated, that someday we'll be living in a quiet house with all kinds of privacy, longing for the days when our children were underfoot. She's right, as usual. By then, if we're blessed, we'll have grandchildren. They'll come to see us every Sunday after church. If it's summer, I'll teach my grandchildren how to make ice cream. They'll ask to turn the handle, and I'll let them. When their skinny arms grow tired, I'll bend down and whisper in their ears what my daddy used to whisper in mine: "Keep going, honey. Anything worth having is worth working for."

When I was younger, I thought the things worth working for were the things I could buy—the big houses and shiny cars. But now I remember how love grew large in that tiny house, how joy came to visit and decided to stay.

The fruit of the Spirit

is love, joy, peace . . .

My Lawn Mower, My Friend

*E*ight years ago, I bought a push mower to cut the grass at my house. We have one acre of ground and cut it from late April through mid-November. If spring comes early or fall lingers, we'll push those boundaries a bit, but for the most part, it's an eight-month-a-year job. By the time I fill the mower with gas, mow the lawn, put string on the trimmer, and whack down all the weeds, I've spent two and a half hours on the lawn. If I have to trim the hedge, it's up to three hours. In the past eight years, I've owned four different string trimmers and three hedge clippers. My faithful mower has soldiered on without a complaint. If mowers go to heaven, mine will trim the grass along the golden streets.

Jack is my neighbor and a member of our Quaker meeting. He came to visit me last fall. I was telling him about my mower, how it's run for eight years and still starts on the first pull—a veritable mower miracle.

"You ought to get that thing serviced," Jack

told me. "Let them clean the carb and check the compression. It's long overdue for a checkup."

He offered some more mower talk, none of which I understood. When he was finished, I had the queasy feeling my mower was pointed graveward. Jack gave me the name of the folks who work on his mower, and the next day I loaded it in the truck and drove down to their shop.

When the lady behind the counter asked me what was wrong with the mower, I told her that I'd used it for eight years and never had it serviced. She said they'd give it a good going-over.

Two weeks later, I got a phone call that my mower was ready. I went back to the shop to retrieve it. The lady told me they'd sharpened the blade and changed the oil and cleaned the carburetor.

"Better than new," she said, with confidence brimming over.

I took it home and started it up. Black smoke belched from the muffler, and oil spewed from the air filter. The engine beat out an irregular rhythm. "Better than new…hack…cough…better than new," it seemed to say.

I put it in my truck and drove back to the shop. The lady was perplexed. She promised they'd make it right. "We'll make it better than new," she yelled after me as I walked out the door. That night at my men's study group, I asked for intercessory prayer for my lawn mower. The next Sunday I preached on advice-giving and how it isn't always welcome. I looked at Jack while I spoke. Guilty as sin of mower malfeasance, and there he was, smiling big and nodding his head.

The lady called me that week to tell me my mower was fixed. I brought it home and started it up. Gasoline poured out onto the garage floor. I turned the mower off and went for a walk. Jack was cutting his grass. He shut his mower off and came over to visit.

"That's my mower," he pointed out. "Seventeen years old. You take care of them, they'll take care of you. How's your mower running? Aren't those people great?"

I went back home to my mower. I sat next to it and thought of the hours we'd spent together. When my wife and I miscarried, I remembered how I'd mowed the yard three times in one week, walking off my sorrow one stripe at a time. A year later, when Joan delivered a healthy boy, I mowed the lawn the day we brought him home from the hospital. I sang and danced the entire acre.

The fault was mine. I had abandoned my mower to people who had wrongly assumed it was just another mower. They didn't know its healing powers. I thought about what Jack had said, how if you take care of them, they'll take care of you. It was time I took care of my mower. There are just some things you shouldn't hire out. I took apart the carburetor and reseated the gaskets. No more gas leak. I drained the oil and put in new, right up to the top of the fill mark. Not a drop more. I backed out the spark plug. It was black and gummy. I went to the gas station and bought a new one. While I was there, I bought premium gas for my mower. Gasoline champagne. I probed the mower's oily recesses with a Q-tip. Then I waxed it to a gleaming shine and sharpened the blade.

I wheeled it outside and pulled the starter cord. One time. It purred to life. "Thank you, thank you, thank you," it called out. I mowed the yard, then pushed it into the garage and wiped it clean. Then we had a little talk, my mower and I. From now on, it's an oil change twice a season and premium gasoline. Sharpen the blade every five acres and lubricate the cable once a year. No more strangers pawing it with their dirty hands. I'm going to take care of my mower, and it's going to take care of me. A fine lesson. I'm glad I've learned it.

Sometimes we want the best from something while giving it our worst. Couples sit in my office and lament their stale marriages, then go home and spend the night in front of the television. I want my sons to confide in me, but I expect them to do it without my showing any interest in their busy little days. We want the stream to pour forth fresh water even as we litter its banks. We want God to be with us round-the-clock, but won't give him the time of day.

Starting now, I'm going to pray while I mow, to see if God and I can't forge a sweeter peace, one stripe at a time.

Bedtime
Stories

Three months before our second son, Sam, was born, we moved Spencer out of the crib and across the hall to a big-boy bed. We'd read that a psychologist told parents not to move one child out of a crib the very day a new baby was put in it. It might cause the older child to resent the younger one. It was all for naught. When we brought baby Sam home, Spencer took one look at him, pointed at my wife's stomach, and said, "Put him back."

When we moved him to his twin-size bed, I got in the habit of lying beside Spencer to tell him a bedtime story. I always tell him about Zipper. Zipper was my dog growing up. We got her when I was a baby. She died a week before I left home at the age of nineteen. After Zipper was gone, I didn't see much point in sticking around.

I tell Spencer how Zipper went fishing with me, how she jumped in the lake to catch a fish that was getting away because she knew times were hard. I told him about the time Zipper and I went camping and how, when we woke up, a deer was sleeping right beside us. None of those things really happened, but they were bedtime stories my father had told me about his dog Zipper, so I'm honor-bound to pass them down the family line.

In the years I've been telling Spencer bedtime stories, I've added a few stories of my own. I tell him how Zipper pulled me from a raging river. Or about the time Zipper bit a charging bull on the nose and saved my life. After I tell him a story, he is full of questions. "How deep was the river? How hard did Zipper bite the bull?" At the age of four, he accepts as gospel truth all I tell him. When he no longer believes me, something precious will be lost. Though I welcome his growth, I do not look forward to that day.

We keep our stereo in his bedroom, high on a shelf, away from little Sam fingers. It is a complicated stereo, one of our few concessions to technological modernity and far too perplexing for Joan and me to figure out. Four-year-old Spencer has it down pat.

When I'm finished telling him about Zipper, Spencer climbs out of bed, runs to the stereo, and plays the Nat King Cole Christmas CD. (I have to remind myself that they're not called records anymore.) Spencer is a serious Nat King Cole fan. He especially likes "Deck the Halls," "Hark! the Herald Angels Sing," and "Joy to the World!" He programs the CD player to perform them in that order. When Spencer is tired, he'll be asleep before Mr. Cole starts tolling the ancient yuletide carol.

My son has little regard for the seasons of music. To his ear, the herald angels sound every bit as good in July as in December. My wife and I sit in our front room on a warm July evening, the windows open, nursing a glass of lemonade, while Nat King Cole sings of peace on earth and mercy mild. It is a fine message, one that bears repeating regardless of season.

The thing I love most about my children is their high regard for the wondrous. Theirs is a world where deer and daddies slumber in peaceful coexistence, where angel bands crowd a meager manger, and life's gravest dangers are bested by a twenty-pound dog with ringworm. There is no incongruity in their world, no jarring clash between fact and fable. All is truth, for now.

But the day will come when things will cease to be true just because Daddy said so. "Is that really true?" will creep into their language. How will we answer our children? Will we tell them that herald angels still sing their advent song? Or that peace on earth and mercy mild are infinitely harder to program than a CD player?

I have friends who tell their toddler son the brutal truth about Santa. I pity the child whose parents so thoroughly rob him of wonder, just as I pity the adult whose cynicism kills the steady beat of an angel's wing. As for me, I believe in what Nat King Cole sings— from herald angels to peace on earth. For truth, like any object of beauty, has many facets. While some things are Zipper-true, others are gospel-true. And each truth has its beauty.

Clyde

ecause we are the parents of two small children, our days are full. Thus we were pleased to come home from Quaker meeting one late-summer Sunday and find the rest of the day luxuriously open, an empty square on the refrigerator calendar.

One hour north is a theme park with kiddie rides and an alligator named Clyde. Though we had never been there, we had driven by the billboards advertising the park. On the billboards, Clyde appears to be twenty feet long, leaping out of a swamp, jaws wide open and fierce. Fury unleashed. After a morning of quiet adoration, the prospect of danger and furor intrigued us. So we called my sister's family to see if they wanted to pay Clyde a visit. My sister is married to a serene man named Tom. They have three small boys who do not share their daddy's tranquil nature. With them, we ventured north to peril.

The theme park is surrounded by September field corn, standing like soldiers, tall and proud before the autumn slaughter. The Ferris wheel rises from their ranks. Our youngest son, Sam, spies it from afar and squeals with anticipation. Like his cousins, he is prone to fits of wild expression. To bring these children together in one place requires myriad patience and prayer. My mother once baby-sat for all five and ended the day a broken woman.

We ride the merry-go-round first. The horses seem bored with their routine and look as if they will bolt were it not for the pole holding them fast. Our four-year-old, Spencer, timid by nature, grips the pole tightly. Sam, on the other hand, rears back in the saddle, flinging his hand in the air. He is eighteen months old and recklessness personified. Joan and I lie awake at night and pray for him, steeling ourselves against the day he starts driving.

The merry-go-round begins a theme. All the rides that follow mimic its circular routine. Rocket ships. Helicopters. Airplanes. Even chickens, glossy purple, orange, and yellow. Chickens with saddles, a combination which has heretofore eluded me. The children, acting as if chickens with saddles are an everyday event, scramble on their backs with nary a stare and ride the chicken circuit. Between rides we savor soft drinks, cotton candy, and huge, melt-in-your-mouth pastries called "elephant ears."

We pass by the kiddie train. Our boys clamor to

ride, but the ride is closed. Just a few weeks before, the
train toppled while rounding a corner and a woman
was crushed to death. The park was closed for a time
while state officials unraveled the mystery of how one
moment a full-of-life grandmother could be holding her
granddaughter, then the next moment lie death-still on
the ground. We clutch our children to us and give the
death train a wide berth.

Clyde the alligator is next. We join the line to see him.
Pictures of him adorn the fence. Clyde thrashing. Clyde
leaping from the swamp, his razor teeth glistening with
blood. In truth, Clyde is four feet long, sits in a murky
concrete puddle, and only moves when a bored employee
tosses a dead chicken over the fence at suppertime. Still,
my timid four-year-old trembles at the sight of him. I,
who had hoped at the very least for a snap of the jaws,
am greatly disappointed. Irony: I visit an alligator looking for danger and find boredom. A grandmother
boards a train to find tranquillity and chances upon
death. What a terrible mystery life can be.

Clyde is the last show of the day. We fold the
strollers and head for home. The children fall asleep.
We carry them in and put them to bed in their clothes.
Spencer stirs and cries out for me to check under his
bed. Clyde is there, he is certain. My assurances to the
contrary are not sufficient. He wants me to lie down
beside him, which I do.

Before long, his breathing evens out. He smells like cotton candy and elephant ears stirred together. I feel his heartbeat. What five minutes before was pulsing and racing, is now settled and subdued. To bring him peace gives me quiet joy.

I continue to hold him, thinking of Clydes and trains and how danger erupts in the oddest places. We spend our lives fencing in lethargic alligators and meet death on a ten-mile-an-hour train. How can parents protect their children in such a senseless world, when danger leaps out from places we scarcely imagine? I pray for strength and courage so that I will not pass on my curious fears to children who have enough of their own. In the darkened room, with legions of alligators underfoot, God draws near and serenity is mine. To bring me peace gives him quiet joy.

Bath
People

A few weeks ago, I was sitting in the bathtub trying to figure out how many baths I have taken. I'm in my mid-thirties and have taken a bath every day of my life. On days I mow the lawn I take two baths. That means I've taken nearly thirteen thousand baths in my lifetime. In all of those years, I have never killed anyone. I wonder if there's a correlation. Maybe we ought to make more bathtubs and fewer bullets.

I grew up in a house with a bathtub. It also had a shower, but we couldn't use it because it leaked down into the kitchen. When I was nineteen, I moved to my own apartment. It didn't have a shower, so I kept taking baths. Then I moved to a farmhouse which didn't have a shower, either. It did have a seven-foot, bright pink bathtub. Sometimes I lie awake at night and think about that tub.

Seven years ago we moved to the house we live in now. It has a shower inside the bathtub, but after a lifetime of baths, the habit is ingrained. You're either a bath person or a shower person, and whichever you are is pretty well determined early in life.

My wife is a shower person. She grew up in a house with a bathtub and a shower. The shower was in their cellar. Her mother didn't want her father coming in from the fields and tracking dirt through the house. So her father tapped into the water pipes and hung a shower head smack in the middle of the cellar next to the furnace. No shower stall. You put your soap and washcloth on a stepladder. The water runs across the cellar floor to the drain. As showers go, it is wonderful. The water comes straight down on top of your head, so you don't have to bend and stoop to get wet like you do in most showers. Still, it is a shower and is therefore inferior to a bath.

Since Sunday through Friday are work days, I have to hurry my bath along. But on Saturday mornings my bath is slow and luxurious. While the water is running, I walk down to the end of the lane to fetch the morning paper. By the time I get back, the water is hot and deep. I lock the bathroom door so the kids can't come in and float boats while I'm reading the paper. The daily news goes down a lot easier when you're soaking in a bathtub. I read about bank robberies and riots in distant cities and it scarcely fazes me. I think to myself how much safer the world would be if folks just stayed home and took a bath. I never feel like rioting or robbing a bank while I'm reclining in the tub.

For years now, I've been trying to sell my wife on the virtues of baths. While showers leave one clean, they also leave a person feeling jangled and edgy. A bath gently laps at your body; a shower pummels and assaults you. My wife smells great, but once a year she battles an ulcer. I'm betting it has something to do with the showers.

The house we live in now is owned by the Quaker meeting I pastor. They've been fixing it up for us. First they fixed the kitchen; then they fixed the basement. Now they want to fix the bathroom. They've formed a committee. All of the persons on the committee are shower people, and I'm starting to worry. They're talking about how much bigger our bathroom would be if we replaced the bathtub with a shower stall. These are ordinarily very nice people, but they're starting to get meddlesome. We've never had a church split, but I can see one coming.

Jesus, I'm pleased to report, was a bath person. Scripture relates how Mary once bathed his feet in perfume. Judas complained that a bath like that was a big waste of money. I bet Judas was a shower person.

For all their benefits, baths can also lead to trouble. Bathsheba, a lovely woman with an even lovelier name, was taking a bath when King David spied her from his rooftop. I'm not going to tell you what happened after that. This is a family book, after all. You can read all about it in 2 Samuel 11. But I warn you—when you're finished reading, you might need to take a cold shower. Unless, of course, you're a bath person.

History
Lessons

My seventh-grade history teacher was Olaf Ellis. Mr. Ellis could be distracted from the day's lesson by asking him to talk about his experiences in World War II. In their own way, his stories were also a history lesson, and certainly more compelling than the presidential election of 1922, which is what we would have studied had not Mr. Ellis been so easily diverted. We would laugh at Mr. Ellis behind his back, thinking ourselves clever for having tricked him out of a lesson. Now I suspect that on the days Mr. Ellis wanted to teach us about the war, he would start by talking about Calvin Coolidge, knowing we would make every effort to steer the conversation warward.

Halfway through the year, I learned that Mr. Ellis had served in the war with my uncle. This was a startling revelation. Every time I visited my uncle, he was sitting in a ponderous chair, chewing an unlit cigar, with his dog in his lap. I could scarcely imagine him charging Omaha Beach while dodging Nazi bullets. Then I reasoned that if he had been in battle, he was now taking a well-deserved rest. My uncle was the only member of our family who had been to war. I so wanted him to be a hero I was willing to give him the benefit of the doubt.

I wondered if the war had cured Mr. Ellis of any flamboyant tendencies he might have possessed in his pre-war years. Probably by the time you go through a war you hope the rest of your life will be routine and nondescript. Mr. Ellis was as predictable as the clock above his classroom door—white shirt, red tie, gray slacks, and a quiz every Friday.

The only thing more difficult than imagining my uncle in battle was imagining Olaf Ellis shooting at someone. Shooting at other people must have gotten to him, for he was a tremendously tender man who seemed bent on pacifying whatever gods he might have offended with his warring. There is a tendency among certain veterans to spend the remainder of their lives rebuilding the world they had once torn asunder. Olaf Ellis was one of these. After the government told him he could stop shooting at people, he came home and taught them; teaching became his medium of restitution.

The Vietnam War was rattling to an end when Mr. Ellis was my teacher. We never talked about Vietnam since it wasn't yet classified as history. I had a current events class, but we didn't talk about it there, either. I come from a people who hope that ignoring tragedy will cause it to disappear. Thus it came as a surprise, to myself as much as anyone, when I became a Quaker pacifist and began marching for peace, raising a loud sign against tragedies of the early 1980s—the proliferation of nuclear bombs and other assorted evils. I might well have been the first person in my town ever to carry a protest sign.

There is no luxury as sweet as youthful certainty. When I was twenty-one, the world's problems were clearly understood and easily resolved. People like Mr. Ellis who went to war were absolutely wrong, and people like me who marched for peace were absolutely right. But then Afghanistan and Burundi and Bosnia came along, and my certainty hit the road. I look at pictures of slain children and catch myself hoping the person who caused their deaths meets a similar end. Such a thought shocks me, for I am, after all and absolutely, a Christian pacifist.

I have laid down my sign. My slogan-truths, my mini-truths, and my shadows of truth have had to make room for other pieces and variations of truth. This causes me great pain. Letting go of past "truth" is like watching your children leave home for good. You know they must depart, but their leaving brings tears.

I am a pacifist not because people are pure and will choose peace if given the chance, for certain folk have their investment in hate, no matter what. I am a pacifist by divine imperative. I am called to a peace that does not collapse when human goodness fails. Rather, it endures, for it is rooted in One whose goodness endures—Jesus Christ—our alpha and omega, our beginning and end.

This peace is not about words on a sign. It is about the Word who became flesh and dwelt among us, full of grace and truth. These are the first casualties in all our wars, both the wars that rage within and the wars that rage without.

The fruit of the Spirit

is love, joy, peace,

patience...

Sally and the Pythagorean Theorem

When I was a sophomore in high school, I had a crush on a girl named Sally. Sally was a cheerleader and a Christian fundamentalist, a curious combination. I fell in love with Sally during geometry. In all my other classes I made C's, but in geometry I made a D, which dashed my dream of a college scholarship. Mr. Gibbs, our principal, called me down to his office when the grades came out.

"Sit down, son," he said. I sat down.

"You made a D in geometry. What's going on?" he asked.

I told Mr. Gibbs I wasn't mathematically inclined, but the real truth was that I spent the whole geometry class smelling Sally's hair. She sat right in front of me. For fifty minutes every day, I concentrated on her blond braids and neglected the Pythagorean theorem.

One Saturday I went to the Rexall drugstore on the town square and sniffed all the shampoo until I figured out what kind Sally used—Herbal

Essence. I bought a bottle and took it home, smelled it, and dreamed of Sally.

Sally was a Baptist. She attended one of the Baptist churches in the next town over. I worshiped at the Quaker meeting, but since my father had grown up Baptist I thought it was time I explored my spiritual roots.

The Baptist Youth Fellowship met on Wednesday nights in their church basement. The first meeting I attended, Sally was there. She was sitting on a couch. I sat down next to her.

Sally said, "Hi, Phil. I didn't know you were interested in God."

"Oh, yes, very interested," I told her. "Very interested."

The lesson that night was led by an eager young seminarian. He wore a T-shirt that read, *Jesus is coming soon. Look busy.*

He began by asking us to confess our sins. Different churches have diverse ideas about what constitutes sin. Since I didn't know the Baptist sins, I had to think back to my Catholic days. According to Father McLaughlin, the two big sins were birth control and eating meat on Friday. So when I thought of sin, that's what came to mind. Thankfully, I was in the clear.

When it came my turn to confess, I said, "No sin here."

The room grew deathly still. The youth leader said quietly, "Everyone sins."

I reassured him, "No, not me. Not this week."

Sally turned to me and quoted the King James Bible: "If we say that we have no sin, we deceive ourselves, and the truth is not in us."

Just to have Sally talk with me was such exquisite pleasure, I scarcely minded that she was calling me a liar. Besides, I hadn't meant to lie, I was just ignorant. I had to go away to college to learn about sin, which is where a lot of folks get their start with it. My German teacher, Sister Marie Pierre, taught me about it. She said sin is anything that turns our hearts away from God. That's when I knew I was a sinner.

The last time I saw Sally was at our high school reunion. She was sitting at the cheerleader table. I gave her a hug and sniffed her hair. It was stiff with hair spray and smelled of chemicals. When she found out I was a pastor, she wanted to talk religion. So we talked about her old Baptist church, which she no longer attends. Too many sinful people there, she told me. Now she goes to one of those churches where sin is something other people do. Somewhere along the way, Sally forgot that sin is inevitable and human perfection an illusion.

As for me, I'm still sinning right along and daily requiring the patient grace of God to make me new.

Though I'm mostly happy, I do have two regrets. I wish the Rexall drugstore were still open, and I wish I had paid a little more attention to the Pythagorean theorem. Along with God's grace, it's the only thing that seems constant these days.

Margaret and Her Pennies

*E*very Monday morning, my friend Jim and I eat breakfast at Bob Evans and swap war stories. Jim pastors an inner-city church, and his stories have more meat and gristle than mine.

One morning he told me about Margaret. Margaret is an eighty-year-old widow in his church. She lives in a retirement center and ventures out once a week to buy groceries at Safeway. Margaret, Jim reports, is a sweet lady, though that hasn't always been the case. She told Jim that when she was younger she was not a good person, but God has slowly changed her. Occasionally, God builds the house overnight, but most times God nails up one board each day. Margaret was a board each day.

Several years ago, Margaret felt God wanted her to do something for her inner-city church. So she prayed about it, and after a while the Lord told her to save all her pennies for the children of the church. Margaret was hoping for something a little grander, but she didn't complain. A person has to start somewhere, she told Jim. So every year at Christmas, she wrapped up her pennies, about ten dollars' worth, and gave them to her church. She told them it was for the kids and not to spend it on pew cushions.

One afternoon a lady down the hall from Margaret came to visit. She noticed Margaret's mayonnaise jar full of pennies. She asked her why she was saving pennies. Margaret told her it was for the kids at church.

"I don't have a church," the lady said. "Can I save up my pennies and give them to the kids in your church?"

"Suit yourself," Margaret said.

Before long, thirty folks in the retirement center were saving their pennies for the kids.

Every Wednesday, they climb on the retirement center's bus and drive to the Safeway. They steer their carts up and down the aisles, then stand in line at the checkout counter. They put their groceries on the moving belt and watch as each price pops up on the display. When the checker calls the total, the old folks count out the money a bill at a time. Then they ask for the change in pennies. They count that out, too, one penny at a time. The other customers stand behind them and roll their eyes. They don't know a work of God is underway.

The next year at Christmastime, the women

loaded up their jars and took their pennies, twenty thousand of them, to the church Christmas party. The kids staggered from the Christmas party, their pockets bursting with pennies.

When the kids found out who was behind the pennies, they wanted to visit the retirement center and sing Christmas carols. Pastor Jim took them in Big Blue, the church bus. They assembled in the dining room. Jim watched from the back row. In front of him sat one of the retirement center ladies. Jim didn't know her, had never seen her. She was explaining to a visitor what was going on.

"These children, you see, they're from our church, and they've come to visit us. We're awfully close."

The next week, one of the men in the retirement center passed away. Jim came and conducted the memorial service right there at the retirement center, which is fast becoming the new church annex.

All of this, mind you, began with Margaret in her apartment praying to the Lord to let her do a mighty work. She admits now that she was a little disappointed when God told her to save her pennies. She was hoping for a more flamboyant ministry. She didn't want to start with pennies. Then she thought back on her own life and how sometimes God builds houses one board each day.

Our Resident Noah

*O*nce when I was between jobs, I worked as a substitute teacher in my hometown. I was a year out of college and most of my former teachers were still around, including Rosemary Helton. She had been hired to teach freshman algebra, but her real purpose was to serve as the town's last line of defense against juvenile delinquency. If a kid made it past Mr. Morris, the junior high shop teacher, with his arrogance intact, Rosemary Helton could guarantee a personality conversion by the Thanksgiving recess.

She was a short, muscular woman given to wearing sweat suits in the classroom. She coached the girls tennis team and would sometimes leave early to make a tennis meet. She'd throw a piece of chalk to Don Dodson and bark, "Dodson, take over!" We would sit and listen while Don Dodson finished the lesson. Don was my friend and a complete flop in other subjects but a wizard at algebra. I was mathematically impaired and would stare open-mouthed while Don said things like, "Obviously, X must equal 24, therefore Y^2 must be 112." Don said "obviously" a lot, though nothing about algebra was ever obvious to me.

Rosemary Helton took me under her sturdy wing. "Gulley," she'd say (she called all of us by our last names), "Gulley, your sister didn't understand this, and neither did your brothers. What is it with your family and math? Here, let me show you." She would hover over me, hammering the gospel of algebra into my head, an evangelist laboring mightily to bring me math salvation.

She never grew discouraged. Toiled forty-plus years to bring enlightenment to our town. Spent her summers praying her next crop of students would produce an Einstein but ended up with a classroom of Forrest Gumps. It was a quirk in our town. We produced a surplus of lawyers but not one mathematician. We felt so guilty about it that we named a street after her, Helton Drive, down at Ellis Park, which was named for Harve Ellis, but that's another story.

Helton Drive starts at the swimming pool, runs by the Little League concession stand, the basketball courts, the drinking fountain, a picnic table, and ends just past the Chuck Brooks memorial tree. Four speed bumps and two stop signs. You can't take it too fast, just like algebra. Teenagers sit at the picnic table and carve dirty words into the wood. It is a testimony to our town's academic excellence that all the words are spelled correctly.

Rosemary Helton is our resident Noah. The Lord told Noah to build a boat, and Noah hammered away for decades, never giving up, never losing faith. Got up every morning, strapped on his tool belt and built himself an ark over the taunts of neighbors who said he'd never use it. (These are the kind of folks who say the same thing about algebra.) Noah would just eye up another nail and drive it home.

Now some people build boats, and others build people. People builders:

...the mother or father whose idea of a good time is reading to the children,

...the social worker who drives a client to the doctor on his day off,

...the teacher whose deepest joy is your moment of "Aha!"

They rise at dawn, say their prayers, and go forth to build their little corner of the kingdom. If Tuesday is bad, they trust Wednesday will be better. They are patient. There is no rush. They are building people, and that takes time.

During the summers, Rosemary Helton hired herself out to teach tennis, ten lessons for five dollars, cheap tuition for the school of Rosemary. I would ride my bike past the tennis courts and listen to her bring another generation along. "Johnson, don't hold your racket that way. Your father had the same problem. What is it with your family and tennis? Here, let me show you."

Now Mrs. Helton is retired, and a whole new batch of teachers are becoming institutions in their own right. I happen upon my old algebra book up in my parents' attic and remember the days when X equaled 24 and Rosemary equaled one patient lady who hammered out a better world, one life at a time.

Town Mottoes

*I*n lieu of mountains and seashores, Indiana has mottoes. Except for my hometown, Danville, which thus far remains motto-free. It isn't because we're without accomplishment—we had the first stoplight in the county—it's because we're a humble people and reluctant to put on airs. Though if we were to brag, we would brag about our town museum, which houses the first postcard ever sent to Danville:

> *Dear Hobart and Edith, We are fine. How are you? Having a great time. Wish you were here. Love, Clarence and Mary. PS We think we left the iron plugged in. Could you check it for us?*

Our town's Civil War regiment flag is in the museum too. The flag is in pristine condition because the men in our town had a notoriously poor sense of direction and ended up spending the Civil War in Toronto.

Some of the people in Danville are tired of our modesty and are talking about putting up a sign out on Highway 36: *Danville: Home of the Civil War Flag.* Someone ran for the town board as a "sign" candidate, and there's talk of a referendum. The churches are even taking up sides. Pastor Thornburg, over at the Quaker church, has been preaching on the virtues of humility and how Jesus was unpretentious and calls us to be the same, while the Episcopalians have been pouring money into the sign movement. The Baptists have been silent, preferring to carry the banner on weightier matters like salvation by faith and baptism by immersion.

Danville is the county seat for Hendricks County, whose motto is "Garden spot of the world." This is a purely subjective claim and one the rest of the world doesn't necessarily acknowledge. Folks in Switzerland don't look at the Alps and say, "Well, they're pretty, but not as pretty as the strip malls of Hendricks County." The beauty in my hometown isn't in the scenery, but in the people.

Of all the town mottoes in Indiana, I like Swayzee's the most. Their motto is "The only town named Swayzee in the entire world!" Swayzee is on State Road 13 in northern Indiana, and they've posted their motto on big signs at the edge of town. I like this motto for its verifiable honesty. A thorough search of an atlas indicates these folks are truth tellers. If my car needed worked on, I would take it to the garage in Swayzee. The bottom of the sign says, *State record-holder for basketball overtimes in one game— nine—1964.* So they're not only honest, they're persistent. And patient. If it takes the boys nine overtimes to finish the game, those people from Swayzee wait it out.

I went to a high school ball game not long ago. Folks were heading for the exits five minutes before the buzzer. This is a new phenomenon in our town that began when advertisers started telling us how busy we are and how time is our most precious commodity. Before that, it was our custom to linger after the game and help Ralph, the janitor, pick things up. Now Ralph is on his own because we're impatient and in a hurry, even if we're only heading home to watch TV.

Impatience is epidemic.

We order clothes from a catalog and pay five dollars extra to get them a day sooner.

We expect children to walk at our pace, not theirs.

And yellow means "speed up" instead of "slow down."

Jesus went to Jerusalem one Passover holiday and met a man who had waited thirty-eight years at the Bethesda pool for a healing. Tradition had it that every so often an angel of the Lord would stir the waters and whoever stepped in first would be cured. For thirty-eight years, this man had reached out for a healing only to be muscled aside by someone bigger and faster.

Some folks say this man didn't want to be healed, or else he would have pushed other folks aside and hustled into that pool himself. I say true patience is so scarce, we're apt to confuse it with apathy. There's a load of difference between the two. Apathy curls up into self-pity when times get hard. Patience quietly waits its turn, trusting that God will get around to making things right in his perfect time.

After this man had been passed over for thirty-eight years, Jesus picked him up and set his feet to Passover dancing. The mills of God grind slowly, but they do grind exceedingly fine. It's a matter of every day dragging yourself one foot closer to the water,

...of not heading home until the buzzer has sounded,

...of remembering how any miracle worth its salt is worth waiting for,

...and trusting that one day an angel of the Lord will stir the water just for you.

I say we paint that on a sign and put it at the edge of town.

Patience, Patience, Patience!!!

When Spencer, our older son, reached two, his normally docile personality turned explosive. One night we tucked Opie into bed; the next morning Charles Manson Jr. awakened. It happened that quickly. We talked it over with friends who have children. One friend told us not to worry about it, that all kids go through that stage. Another friend said it was time to fake our deaths and pass our kids off to my sister.

We went to the library and checked out books on child rearing. They didn't help much. Mostly they talked about whether it is ever appropriate to raise your hand against a child. I appreciate Robert Orben's advice on this matter: Never raise your hand against a child; it leaves your midsection unprotected.

We have a friend who's a social worker. One Sunday morning after worship, she gave us a handful of child-rearing pamphlets. We took them home to read. They were very helpful in preparing us for what we might expect down the road from our kids, besides nervous exhaustion and poverty.

We put the pamphlets in a cabinet and forgot about them. A couple of years later, we came across them while spring cleaning. Spencer was four, and Sam was two. The pamphlets told us that four-year-olds like adventure and have active minds. That certainly was true of Spencer. Just the week before, he had tied Sam to the toilet and locked the door. The pamphlets also said four-year-olds have a tendency to lie and use swear words. So basically, what we have is a lying cusser with a penchant for knot-tying. Sounds like the Boy Scouts in my hometown when I was growing up.

I didn't get discouraged. I'm looking to the future. Spencer will turn five before long. Five-year-olds, the pamphlets report, are sunny and serene. They like being near their mothers and are eager to help. I'm all for that. We can start with the supper dishes. They also say five-year-olds are quiet. We're looking forward to that. Unfortunately, Sam will be three then. Three-year-olds are on the loud side, the pamphlets tell us. I wonder if there'll ever be a time when they're both in a quiet stage at the same time.

Sam is two now. Tense, explosive, and rigid, the pamphlets confide. Yep. Bossy, demanding. Check. I read on. If your two-year-old gets out of hand, it is appropriate to discipline him. You can correct the child by placing him in timeout for two minutes. Do not put the child in a bedroom or closet, the pamphlet cautions. A closet? Isn't it sad that you have to warn parents not to put their kids in a closet? Any savvy parent would never leave kids in a closet for two minutes; otherwise, they'll pull all the clothes down and you'll have to iron them again.

When Sam misbehaves, we put him in his crib for two minutes, a minute for each year of his age— though according to the pamphlet, timeout in a bedroom is harmful to the child. I don't understand why. I'd carry on all the time if it meant I got to lie quietly on my bed for thirty-six minutes.

The parents of a two-year-old must have patience, advises the pamphlet. Patience is written in big, bold letters. It leaps from the page. PATIENCE, PATIENCE, PATIENCE!!!

Sam pulls the ketchup from the refrigerator and squirts it all over the kitchen. Patience. He knocks over a lamp; the lightbulb shatters; there are no spare lightbulbs in the house. Patience. He takes a pail of water and dumps it on the bathroom floor; it leaks through to the freshly drywalled basement ceiling. Patience.

What I give to my children, God returns fourfold. This patience runs two ways. God reads the pamphlet for thirty-six-year-old fathers. Temperamental, it says.

Cranky. Need security. Self-centered. Yes, all those things and more. Treat with patience, the pamphlet counsels. PATIENCE, PATIENCE, PATIENCE!!!

My wife and I are praying about whether we should have more than two children. We've asked God to give us a sign. Keep an eye peeled for flying donkeys.

The fruit of the Spirit

is love, joy, peace,

patience, kindness . . .

Warts
and All

In the fifth grade, I fell madly in love with a new girl named Barbara. She had moved to our town from the city and possessed a sensual, sophisticated glamour I found most alluring. We sat alphabetically, and since her last name began with a *D* and mine with a *G*, she was placed next to me.

I would sit in my chair and inhale Barbara's perfume, thanking God I was born to a man named Gulley and not Zelinski. David Zelinski sat four rows away, also awash in love, bemoaning his cruel fate. Halfway through the year, Barbara's stepfather adopted her, her last initial changed from *D* to *W*, and she moved four rows over next to David. Thus was David's faith in a benevolent God reborn, while I teetered on the edge of atheism.

This was the first in a chain of curses during what turned out to be a Job-like year. On the heels of her name change, I contracted a virus which caused twenty-six warts to grow on my hands. On

Sunday mornings at Saint Mary's, I would lift my wart-roughened hands heavenward and implore God to heal my affliction. On Mondays, Barbara would steal glances at my hands, speculating on what repulsive deed I must have done to merit such a leprous condition.

Doctor Kirtley spoke of a miracle worker in the city, a man who burned warts off. My mother drove me to his office, where he painted my warts with his formula. Within a week my warts fell off, though in a month's time they grew back even more profusely, much like a meadow razed by fire regenerates fourfold a season later. Then Doctor Kirtley sent us to a man who froze my warts off. I had to wear bandages on my hands for several weeks. I would stand Napoleon-like on the playground, my bandaged hands thrust under my jacket. That cure, too, was short-lived, and I resigned myself to a life of privation.

The summer following that horrific year, my father took me to visit Harve Ellis. Mr. Ellis worked at the town park and enjoyed a reputation as a man of virtue. My father was forever dragging me to meet people like Mr. Ellis, hoping their Christian values would rub off on me. Today, I return to my hometown and old-timers talk about Mr. or Mrs. Such-and-So and then say, "You probably don't know who I'm talking about; they were before your time." But I always remember and can tell of Saturday mornings on front-porch swings while Judge Helton and Harve Ellis and Lorena Rutledge dispensed their timeless wisdom.

The Saturday I met Mr. Ellis, he shook my hand and then said, "I notice you have warts."

"Thirty-five of them," I told him, "and increasing by the week."

He eyed me up and down, then pulled a fifty-cent piece from the chest pocket of his overalls. "I'll buy them from you," he said. What an odd thing. My parents had spent upwards of a hundred dollars to have my warts removed, and Mr. Ellis wanted to pay fifty cents for them. I took the half-dollar from his work-worn hand.

"Keep that money," he instructed, "and when your warts go away, use that same money to buy someone else's warts."

By the time our county fair came, my warts had vanished. Incredible, but true. I prowled the midway looking for Barbara, eager to make myself available for hand-holding if she had a mind to. But that summer she was holding hands with David Zelinski. Still, to be wart-free was such a blessing that her indifference scarcely mattered.

When I recall how Mr. Ellis brought me back into the human fold, I remember that Jesus once took ten lepers in hand and did the same. For years, they'd stood outside looking in. Then with a touch and a word and a healing, Jesus unlatched the gate and welcomed them home. Kindness is always looking to swing wide the mercy gate.

Mr. Ellis died the next year. I tucked the fifty-cent piece away in a box, and every now and again I pull it out to hold it. I've read somewhere that warts are genetic, so I'm saving it against the day my sons' warts stand betwixt them and their Barbaras.

Just before Mr. Ellis died, we named the park for him. I drive by and recall a Saturday morning, long ago, when a kind old man took an awkward young boy in hand and gifted him with a healing, warts and all.

Kindness
Bestowed

Right before I was born, my parents bought a house on Martin Drive in one of our town's first subdivisions. No front porch, no trees, just a cookie-cutter box on a postage-stamp lawn. Still, the neighborhood had its charms. We lived next door to Mark Nickerson, the town's oddest child. Mark would eat dirt out of our flower beds. He'd come home from school, his mouth ringed with white dust from gnawing on chalk. Mom said Mark was probably lacking something in his diet, though his diet seemed fine to me. Every morning his mother fed him cupcakes and Coke. I would stand at their front door, peering through the screen, imploring them to invite me in for breakfast.

Around the corner from us lived the Wrights and the Chalfants. Mr. Wright sold Knapp shoes and had a sign in front of his house inviting folks to come in and try on a pair. One day Mr. Wright caught a snapping turtle that had wandered into his yard and invited us to his house the next day for turtle soup. He was all the time cooking up any wildlife unfortunate enough to cross his path. After a while the beasts of the field learned to cut a wide swath around his home. Dale Chalfant worked with his dad, Lemmie, in the plumbing business. Dale would walk over to our house once a month and sit in the kitchen with a towel over his shoulders while my mother cut his hair. In exchange, Dale would unclog our pipes for free.

The Myerses and the Blaydeses resided two empty lots away. I'll never forget how my mom and Mrs. Blaydes stood in those lots holding each other and crying the day the Myers boy got killed on his motorcycle on North Salem Road. Inabelle Keen was a nurse and in her off-hours mended our scrapes. She would reach deep in her black bag and paint us with various healing balms. But when the Myers boy died, not even Inabelle Keen and her black bag could set things right.

Mr. and Mrs. Bolton lived down the street from us with their two sons. On summer evenings, Mr. Bolton would back his car out of his garage, set up his reel-to-reel projector and screen, arrange three rows of folding chairs, and show cartoons to the neighborhood kids. He would wear a path between the kitchen and garage, plying us with popcorn and soda pop. We would sit in the folding chairs and watch Mickey and Pluto and Donald.

We moved from that neighborhood when I was eight

years old. Even then I knew that Mr. Bolton and Inabelle Keen were rare birds; the chances my new neighborhood would duplicate them were slim. Sure enough, there were no more summer-evening cartoons in a garage, no more balms in black bags, no more turtle soup. Still, other acts of kindness were bestowed: the widow Bryant and her snickerdoodle cookies, Mrs. Harvey doling out Juicy Fruit, Lee and Mary Lee Comer wallpapering our kitchen the year of the blizzard.

Not long ago I was lamenting how kindness is a relic. If an old man invites neighborhood kids to watch cartoons, we suspect evil things of him. Emergency rooms have taken the place of the Inabelle Keens. Folks who hang wallpaper are found in the Yellow Pages, not next door.

But then I remembered how when our apple trees needed trimming, Mr. Austin broke out his saw. When my sons were short a football, Mrs. Evens across the street came up with a spare. When the days were hot, the Bakers opened their pool. When my faucet was leaking, Mr. Stewart came to our door with his magic wrench. When we came back from vacation, Ray Davis had mowed our lawn. And when our little boy Spencer was operated on, Denise and Dolores from church cried in the waiting room.

A long time ago, Elijah the prophet hermited himself away in a cave and moaned to God how rotten the world had turned. But God knew differently and spoke of thousands of virtuous folk he was proud to call his own.

Kindness thrives. It's awareness that's on the wane.

Sister
Rosalie

When I was six, my mother went to work as a schoolteacher at a Catholic school in the next town over. The school sat next to the Catholic church. When the church was built, they hung a large fish symbol on the outside wall. For several years I thought my mother worked at a bait and tackle shop.

The other teachers were nuns. One of them was named Sister Rosalie, a hardy, humorous woman. She taught first grade. This was back in the days before mandatory kindergarten, so for many children Sister Rosalie was their first exposure to formal education. To this day, there are people in that town who sit up straight and clasp their hands when a nun enters the room.

The summer of my seventh year, my brother David underwent a hernia operation. Sister Rosalie came to baby-sit while my parents were at the hospital. The rest of us kids were deeply concerned, especially after my brother Glenn pointed out that David would get to recuperate on the couch for a solid week and pick the TV shows. Mistaking our worried expressions for sibling compassion, Sister Rosalie went to the kitchen to bake us a cake.

We were playing in the side yard when a muffled boom shook our house. We watched as the back screen door blew open and our cat streaked out, its fur blown off and whiskers singed. Sister Rosalie staggered out behind our cat, clutching her cross, her hosiery melted from her legs and hanging in shreds.

We had been having problems with our stove. The pilot light would go out. My mother would open the door, air out the room, then strike a match and relight the stove. Unfortunately, she forgot to relay that procedure to Sister Rosalie, and when the sister struck a match in a kitchen filled with gas, our stove was blasted to the heavens.

The year was 1968. Some people remember 1968 as the year of the Chicago riots and widespread national upheaval. The people of Martin Drive remember 1968 as the year a cake-baking nun almost blew our block to smithereens. We found our cat the next day in Charlie Schneider's garage. She was huddled in a box, as disheveled as the war protesters in Chicago. We took her home, but she was never the same. Whenever nuns would come to visit, our cat would cower in a far corner and howl, tormented by feline flashbacks.

Several years after the explosion, Sister Rosalie left

the classroom to become a hospital chaplain in the city. Now, when people in my Quaker meeting are sick, I visit them at the hospital where she ministers. On my way to their rooms, I stick my head in her office and holler "Boom!" Then I tell her coworkers all about 1968. I get the feeling Sister Rosalie wishes I'd take a job somewhere else.

Every year the nuns from the Catholic school hold a reunion at my parents' home. On their dining room wall hangs a family picture which was taken in 1968. Sister Rosalie looks at that picture, turns to my mother, and says, "That's how I remember your kids." I remember her standing on our back porch with singed hair and melted hosiery.

Next to my Grandma Norma, I think Sister Rosalie is the first saint I ever met. I've studied up on saints. Saints are people whose love for God causes them to do kind things even if they're dangerous. That pretty well describes baby-sitting.

Once when I was at the hospital, I saw Sister Rosalie comforting a patient, holding his hand and praying with him. I didn't yell "Boom!" then. I just stood and watched a saint in action and thought back to 1968 when all the world seemed crazy except for Grandma and Sister Rosalie.

My parents kept that stove another ten years. Forever after its broiler drawer hung askew, mute testimony to that turbulent year. Sister Rosalie, however, stood steady as an oak. That is what faith steeped in kindness can do.

Consider
the Birds

Our meetinghouse sits on ten acres of land, half of it wooded. Early one spring, as I walked down the meetinghouse lane on my way to the office, I saw a duck waddle out of the woods and across the lawn. While ducks often fly over the premises, it is unusual to see one gadding about on the ground.

The next Sunday we held an Easter egg hunt for the children in our congregation. Twenty screaming children were loosed on the grounds in search of eggs. The duck emerged from the woods, curious about this human invasion. Her eyes were bugged out, her duck walk slow and tentative. A toddler spied her nest of eggs and wobbled in her direction. The duck rocketed back to her nest, her feathers raised and ruffled.

We gathered around. Duck eggs—what a surprise! Smack-dab in the heart of the city, four off-white eggs tucked inside a hollowed beech tree. It brought out the naturalist in us. We wracked our brains, straining to recall everything we'd ever heard about duck eggs.

One of our members is Korean. "In Korea, they eat duck eggs," she told us. The children gaped at her, horrified at that revelation.

"They also eat dogs," she said. The children looked around for their mothers. This was not the kind of cultural exchange we had hoped for when she began attending our Quaker meeting.

The toddler boy had touched one of the eggs.

"We might as well destroy those eggs," one man said. "Once the mother smells that human scent, she'll abandon the whole lot of them."

I had read somewhere that birds do that, though I wasn't sure it was true. We thought about that for a while but decided against it when no volunteer stepped forward to do the squashing. This is the problem with pastoring a bunch of Quaker pacifists. We can't agree whether or not to set mousetraps in the meetinghouse.

Before long, the theological ramifications were being debated. The man who had suggested destroying the eggs pointed out that God has given us dominion over the birds of the air and the beasts of the field. A woman quoted the Bible about how God has known us since we were in our mothers' wombs, and if that's true for us, then why not for ducks?

"But do ducks have wombs?" someone asked. We weren't sure.

We looked around for Mac. Mac attends our meeting and knows a great deal about nature. He is a self-taught expert on a range of topics, from duck wombs to water heaters. Mac told us to leave the duck and her eggs alone. He said that sometimes you just have to trust a duck to do the right thing.

The next morning the duck peered at me from the woods. In midweek I went to check on the eggs. One was missing. Raccoon, I thought to myself. The next day I checked the eggs again. They were gone. Fragments of shell littered the ground around the nest. I talked with Mac about it. He thought maybe the eggs had hatched and the mother had spirited her ducklings away. I found myself wishing it were true. In the short week I'd known the duck, I'd grown fond of her. That night I prayed for her and her young brood. I'd never prayed for a duck before, though I once beseeched the Lord on behalf of a schnauzer.

I didn't tell anyone I had prayed for the duck. My theological reputation is already shaky. But I don't think it's far-fetched to believe that the God who fusses over us extends the same tender consideration to birds of the air and beasts of the field. Remember how Jesus pointed out God's care for dime-a-dozen birds? And if that's true for birds, then it's doubly true for ducks and cats and dogs. Except maybe for poodles, which are proof positive that not everything in creation has a purpose.

The Day I Met Paul Harvey

*D*enise is a member of our Quaker meeting. She has a sister named Dina who moved to Chicago and fell in love with Paul Harvey Jr., the son of the famous radio commentator. Then Dina and Paul Jr. came to visit Denise, and she brought them to church. After meeting for worship, Paul Jr. said he liked my message. A year or so later he and Dina sent some of my stories to a man in the publishing business, and a year after that, my first book, *Front Porch Tales*, hit the bookstores. Paul Jr. wrote the foreword and Mr. Harvey talked about it on his radio program.

One day I was in Chicago on business with my friend Stan. I remembered Paul Jr.'s address and decided to stop in to say hello and thank him for his help. It was lunchtime, so Paul Jr. invited us to stay and eat. "We're having tuna salad sandwiches," he said. "Is that okay?"

My parents had taught me to eat what was put before me, so I said tuna salad was fine. Truthfully, tuna salad is not my favorite food, but since we hadn't told him we were stopping by, I didn't feel I should be picky.

Stan said, "I really don't care for tuna salad. Do you have anything else?" I wanted to slap him.

Then Paul Jr. said, "We eat lunch with my mother and father, so we need to go next door." I've listened to Paul Harvey on the radio all my life. My father has listened to him for the past forty years. Now Stan and I were walking across his yard to have lunch with him.

We went to the living room to wait for Mr. Harvey. There was a Bose Wave radio on the table. Mr. Harvey's been telling us for years how wonderful they sound. Paul Jr. turned it on for me. We listened to a guy named Monty Vonny, or something like that. He's not from these parts, so I'd never heard of him. The only Monty I knew was Monty Chadwick, who owned the Jiffy Carwash back in my hometown of Danville. But it was pretty music. I may save up and buy one of his CDs.

Then Mr. Harvey walked in the room. He looked at me and said, "Well, I'll be; Phil Gulley is standing in my living room. I can't believe it!"

I couldn't believe it, either. I shook his hand and introduced him to Stan.

"Is this the guy who doesn't like tuna salad?" he asked, pointing to Stan.

"The same," I answered.

Mr. Harvey asked me if I liked that Monty Vonny fellow. I told him I didn't know, I'd never met him. Then I told him all about Monty Chadwick and the Jiffy Carwash. If Mr. Harvey ever comes to Danville, we're going to take our cars there and get them washed. My treat, I told him. They've added a foaming brush that really gets the dirt off. Mr. Harvey said he's looking forward to it.

We ate in the breakfast nook just off their kitchen. Stan ate chicken salad and toasted cheese. I ate my tuna salad. They put three of those little tomatoes on my plate, but I didn't eat them. Tomatoes make me burp, and I didn't want to do that in front of Mr. Harvey. I sat next to him and told him about the people in my little Quaker meeting. He told me how he got his start in radio. He is one of the kindest men I've ever met.

After lunch we sat around the table and visited awhile. Then it was time to go. They walked us out to our car. As we drove away, Stan turned to me and said, "I can't believe we just ate lunch in Paul Harvey's kitchen."

I said, "I can't believe you told them you didn't like tuna salad."

He said, "I can't help it. I've been a Quaker too long. I tell the truth without even thinking about it."

I told him it was obvious he wasn't thinking.

As famous as Mr. Harvey is, I wasn't too nervous about meeting him. I've been around famous people before. I met Michael Landon back when he was Little Joe on *Bonanza* and came to Danville to give a speech on the courthouse lawn. I was six years old and remember being mad he didn't bring his horse.

My cousin, Matt Griffith, once dated a beauty queen from Florida. She was Miss Navel Orange of 1972. He brought her to our house for a visit. She was wearing a sash and a crown topped with a gold orange. She signed a Sunkist for me, but the next day my brother Glenn ate it for breakfast.

Here's what I learned about famous people. Most of them are wonderful human beings, because somewhere along the line, someone gave them a leg up and they remember that. At least the good ones do. When Paul Harvey was fourteen years old, his teacher took him in hand and introduced him to the folks at the local radio station. Over half a century later, he remembers it still.

None of us ever got anywhere except through the kindness of others. Sometimes we boast about being self-made, but that's just a lie we tell ourselves to feel important. We're all indebted to someone.

Next time you're driving by the house of someone who has done you a good turn, knock on his door and thank him. He'll appreciate it. Who knows, you might even be offered a tuna salad sandwich. If you are, sit down and eat it. And be sure to put the napkin on your lap instead of tucking it into your shirt collar like my friend Stan did. Boy, I can't take that guy anywhere.

The fruit of the Spirit is love, joy, peace, patience, kindness, goodness. . .

The Crime Wave

Crime has seldom been a problem in my hometown, except once during my teenage years when several houses were burglarized. The robbers would back their truck up to a house, load up, and drive away. During that same time, Norwood Roberts claimed to have been mugged outside the Elks Lodge, though it later turned out he had lost his money in a poker game, didn't want to tell his wife, so concocted a wild story about a hoodlum stealing his money. Still, all of this was enough to make us watch one another a little closer.

It was during this period of paranoia that my father noticed a strange truck backed up to Mrs. Draper's house. Mrs. Draper was our widow neighbor and was visiting out of town. Dad called Charlie, our town's police officer. Charlie had been hoping for a lucky break in the case and hurried over to my dad's house to look the situation over. He parked his cruiser three doors down, slipped up to my parents' home, consulted with Dad, then inched over to Mrs. Draper's house, his holster unsnapped and his gun at the ready.

Past the hedge, around the house, through the back door. Paused to listen. Heard a sound in the basement. Stealthed down the stairs, close to the wall so the steps wouldn't creak. Pitch dark. He saw a flashlight beam right past the furnace, over by the laundry sink.

Stealing a widow's washer and dryer—what is this world coming to? Charlie wondered.

He saw a flash of metal, possibly a gun. He raised his pistol and fingered the trigger.

"Drop it," he ordered. "I have a gun." So Frank, the town plumber, dropped his wrench. He would have yelled, but Frank is a steady man, not prone to outbursts. Though lately Frank had been edgy, having heard about Norwood getting mugged and suspecting in a fatalistic kind of way that he was next on the list. Now here he was, down in a dark basement fixing pipes, Mrs. Draper two states away. They wouldn't find his body for days. What a way to go.

Frank turned to face his attacker. Confront your danger like a man, his father had taught him. Go down fighting.

"Frank, is that you?"

"Charlie, what are you doing here?"

So Charlie told him, and they talked a little bit

about Norwood and the crime wave and wasn't it a shame and did Charlie have any clues. Talked for nearly half an hour, with my dad over on his front porch wondering what in the world those robbers were doing to poor Charlie. He was just about to round up a posse when Frank and Charlie came out and stood by Frank's new truck, which Frank hadn't gotten around to painting his name on yet.

Charlie never did find those robbers. The story going around was that someone from the city was picking us clean. When you live in a small town, it's tempting to blame every evil on ne'er-do-wells from the city. The alternative is believing one of your own did it, which is probably the case, but too painful to consider. Denial does a thriving business in the average small town. Like when Norwood's wife found his wallet in the mop bucket, which is where he had hidden it after the poker game. She never said a word, preferring ignorance over enlightenment. Easier to think he was mugged than face the truth that her gentle Norwood had a shadow side.

This denial of our shadow side is understandable, though most unhelpful. It is when we acknowledge our capacity for evil that we're better able to bring shadow into light. Truth is, we're a mixed-bag people. Consider this:

...the King David who struck up the band in

praise to God is the same David who killed a man after sleeping with his wife;

...the Saint Peter who wore martyr chains with joy is the same Peter who swore Jesus was a stranger;

...the kid who sacked your groceries and called you "ma'am" is the same kid who took your television.

Their condition is our condition. We practice goodness, and we scurry after evil. Jekyll and Hyde. Mixed bag. King David and Saint Peter and sacker-boy. That's us. No denying it. Just ask Charlie; he'll confirm it. He knows our seamy side.

Back in Danville we still leave our doors unlocked, though some days we wish we hadn't. Ninety-nine per-cent of us you can trust, but watch out for that one percent. Depending on the day, it could be any one of us. God isn't finished with our town yet. We're not all saints. We each have our shadow side, and some of us linger there a little longer than we should.

Bernice

While I was in college, I pastored a little Quaker meeting in the country. The first Sunday I was there, Edith Record stood and asked us to pray for her friend Bernice. Bernice's tongue had turned a painful black. We'd never prayed for anyone with a tongue condition but were open to the idea. Bernice went to Doctor Bradley, who peered at her and told her she had an affliction known as black, hairy tongue. He told her to rub baking soda on her tongue then rinse her mouth with peroxide once a day until she was better.

After a few weeks she wasn't any better, so her family took her to the Mayo Clinic, where they poked and prodded Bernice for three days. Then they made their diagnosis: black, hairy tongue. They told her they could give her medicine, but the best cure was to rub baking soda on it once a day then rinse her mouth with peroxide until she was better.

Bernice told me all about it when I went for a

visit after her trip to Mayo. "I knew all along Doctor Bradley was right. It was my kids' idea to go to the Mayo Clinic," she said. Bernice went along with it because she was bored at home and a trip to the Mayo Clinic seemed an interesting diversion.

Three months later Edith Record asked us to pray for Bernice's tongue again. "It's still a painful black," she reported. By that time we were old hands at praying for sore tongues, so we prayed with gusto.

Bernice had a daughter named Betty. Betty had a medical book that listed every ailment known to man. She read it whenever she needed perking up. Contemplating all the things that can go wrong with us but don't can have a cheering effect. After long nights of reading, Betty found something called pernicious anemia that turns your tongue black and makes it hurt. She took her mother back to Doctor Bradley, who ran a blood test and discovered Bernice had pernicious anemia. He hadn't tested for it earlier because it's quite rare. Bernice didn't hold it against him. "He's every bit as good as the doctors at Mayo," she told people.

In addition to her anemia, Bernice was going deaf and blind. Once I was walking up her sidewalk and could hear her radio turned on full blast. She was sitting in her rocking chair, the radio pressed to her ear, listening to a basketball game. She was a fan of Indiana University basketball and Coach Bobby Knight. When Coach Knight threw a chair during a basketball game, they showed it on TV. Bernice told me it was trick photography. Bobby Knight said he saw an old lady standing up who needed a chair so he threw her the one he was using. That might have been Bernice.

Shortly after that, I moved away and lost track of Bernice. Then one day her daughter, Betty, called to tell me that Bernice had died and asked if I would conduct the funeral. Bernice and her husband, Adelbert, had moved from their hometown in 1928. When he died in 1977, he was buried back in their hometown cemetery. We took Bernice back there to rest beside him.

We drove thirty-five miles to reach Bernice's hometown. She'd been gone from there nearly seventy years, but the townspeople still pulled over when the hearse drove by. The men doffed their seed-corn caps. The fire department had blocked traffic at the town's stoplight so the funeral procession would have a clear path. The fireman stood beside the fire engine, his hands clasped and head bowed. You can tell a lot about a town by what it does when a hearse passes through.

Bernice was buried in the same graveyard as her mother, who died in the flu epidemic of 1918 when Bernice was eight. Bernice got shifted from one relative to another until she married Adelbert and moved away. They had a daughter named Fleta who died at the age of eighteen. Bernice never told me all these things. Mostly she just talked about her blessings. She lost her mommy, lost her daughter, lost her husband, lost her hearing, lost her sight, but spoke of blessings. You can tell a lot about people by what they do when pain passes through.

There are all kinds of learning in this world. There are the things you learn at college, such as science and poetry and math. Then there are the things you learn sitting in Bernice's front room, such as prayer and goodness and faith.

Annice

When I was young and unattached, the women in my Quaker meeting paid me considerable attention. But then Quaker women tend to take an inordinate interest in people who need help. And I needed help. I was six feet tall and weighed 110 pounds. One of the women, Annice, took me on as a project.

One Sunday after worship, she approached me. "Steve," she said, "why don't you come to my house for dinner?" Steve wasn't my name, but for as long as I knew Annice, that's what she called me. When I tried to explain my name was Phil, she told me there was nothing wrong with the name Steve and I should be proud of it. After all, Stephen was the first Christian martyr. Annice was a retired missionary and had a high opinion of Christian martyrs.

Annice had taught at the Quaker girls school in Ramallah, Jordan. During the Six Day War, an Israeli tank commander drove his tank into the school's compound. Annice stood with her hands on her hips and blocked his way. When he stuck his head out of the turret, Annice ordered him to leave immediately.

"Shame on you," she told him. "Shame on you for fighting. What would your mother think?"

The battle-hardened tank commander, more accustomed to soldiers than to sixty-year-old Quaker missionaries from Indiana, looked Annice up and down, climbed back in his tank, and drove away. I didn't know this about Annice until after she died, when one of her nephews told the story during her memorial service. But from what I knew of Annice, it seemed to fit.

Annice lived next to the meetinghouse. She invited me home every Sunday after Quaker meeting for pot roast and peas. The meat was invariably tough and leathery, the peas burnt. Annice would hover over me while I ate, telling me to clean my plate because people in Africa didn't have any food. Once I suggested that we mail them her pot roast. It probably would have kept.

"Don't be ungrateful, Steve," she said. "No one likes a smart aleck. That's probably why you're not married yet."

Annice wasn't married either, but I didn't dare point that out.

In the Quaker faith, if you want to be a pastor, others first have to notice your gifts for ministry. It isn't enough to say you feel called to it. Annice was the first person to tell me I should be a pastor.

"Steve," she said, "I think you should become a pastor."

I told her I didn't feel called to the pastoral ministry. She drew herself up, put her hands on her hips (it was the Six Day War all over again), and said, "Do you know what calling is? Calling is when you see something that needs done, so you do it. We need pastors, so you should do it."

I promised her I would pray about it. I really didn't want to be a pastor, but by then it was too late; Annice had already made up my mind. Since I was engaged to be married, I told my fiancée that Annice wanted me to be a pastor.

She asked, "Why don't you tell her you don't want to be a pastor?"

"I've been trying for five years to tell her my name isn't Steve. I don't think it'll do any good," I said.

So I quit my job and went away to college for eight years and became a pastor. I figured it would be easier in the long run.

Annice came to hear my first sermon. She walked up to me after I'd finished speaking.

"Steve, maybe I was wrong," she said.

Sometimes we think that being a Christian means

being nice. Annice never subscribed to that notion. Beneath her gruff exterior was a woman who meant every word she said. She wasn't interested in being nice; she was interested in doing good, and she tried never to confuse the two.

Even after I married, I continued to join her for Sunday dinner. I'd go to visit and would have to stand; her chairs were piled high with clothing for refugees half a world away.

"Steve, if you want to be a pastor, you're going to have to do better," she'd say.

"My becoming a pastor was your idea," I would point out.

"There you go again, being a smart aleck. Why don't you make yourself useful and take me to the post office to mail off these clothes?"

I stayed at Annice's Quaker meeting for five years, then moved on. But scarcely a day passes that I don't wish folks cared more about doing good than being nice.

When Annice died, I returned to her Quaker meeting for the memorial service. One man stood and told how Annice had taught him to read. Cassie Swarn from the A.M.E. church down on Vine Street talked about how sometimes Annice showed up at her church, a lone white face in a sea of black and brown. She came for the music, Cassie said. Annice liked her music robust. It pained her to sit in the meetinghouse and listen to our feeble attempts at singing, so twice a year she worshiped at the A.M.E. church.

Annice has been gone for over ten years. Whenever I eat pot roast I think of her and clean my plate.

A Tribute to
Ned Ludd

I was talking with a friend about computers and the information superhighway. Like most computer evangelicals, my friend won't be happy until everyone has one. I don't own a computer and told him I have no intention of buying one. The only highway I want to travel is a dogwood-laden road deep in Posey County.

"You're a Luddite," he told me.

"What's a Luddite?" I asked him.

"If you had a computer, you could look it up," he said.

I went home and looked it up in my Webster's dictionary. There it was, sandwiched between "Lucullan" and "ludicrous." "Luddite: one of a group of early 19th century English workmen destroying laborsaving machinery as a protest; one who is opposed to technological change." The Luddites were named for Ned Ludd, a textile worker who correctly perceived a weaving machine to be a threat to his livelihood. So in 1811 he took sledgehammer in hand and beat the machine to pieces. Ned Ludd is my hero.

My brother Glenn recently bought a computer. He called me on the phone, wanting my e-mail address.

"What's an e-mail address, and why do you want it?" I asked him.

"So we can talk on our computers," he said.

"I don't have a computer," I told him. "I have a phone. Why can't we talk on that?"

My mailman, Charlie, says he's holding on to his job by a thread, a modern-day Ned Ludd.

"It's the computers," he tells me. "Everyone's sending e-mail. Nobody's writing letters anymore."

He doesn't like fax machines, either. I bought a fax machine a few months back, and haven't been able to look Charlie in the eye since.

In my kitchen sits an antique cupboard. On the bottom shelf is a shoe box filled with letters. There's one from my Grandma Norma, now absent from this world. Scratchy, old-woman writing, congratulating me for graduating from high school in 1979. It overflows with praise, as if I'd graduated number one from Harvard. She sent me twenty dollars, too. Can't remember what I spent it on. But I bet it didn't bring me the joy that Grandma's letter brings me every time I open the shoe box and see it there. If our house ever caught on fire, I'd grab my wife, my kids, and my shoe box, in that order.

Can people save their e-mail in a shoe box? Will they pass it down to their children, like I'll pass Grandma's letter down to my sons?

"This was from your great-grandmother Norma. Didn't she have beautiful writing? They called it the Palmer method. They used to teach that in school."

Today's kids learn the keyboard; twenty years from now we'll be reminiscing over the dot matrix and laser printer. It won't be the same.

Friends, here's a little encouragement. Go buy the finest pen and paper you can afford. If you have to go a day or two with an empty wallet, it'll be worth it. Set aside a quiet hour one evening after the kids are in bed, and write someone a letter. Tell her how much you love her, how proud she makes you, how her friendship means more to you than anything in the world. I'll make you a promise. When she dies and her children are sorting through her belongings, they'll come across that letter tucked away in a shoe box. The paper will be creased from its many readings. The children will tell you that when their mother was discouraged, she went to the shoe box, read that letter, and brushed away a tear.

Ned Ludd was right. These new ways aren't always the best ways, and before we embrace them, we'd better be sure we know what it is we're giving up.

The Information Line

Over the course of my life, I've had ten different jobs. The best job was doing lawn maintenance during the summers of my college years. My boss was named Louie. He was short and sturdy, a squat oak of a man and the best boss I ever had. Louie told you what to do then left you alone to do it. Entire weeks passed without Louie calling me into his basement office. When he did, it was to pay me a compliment and offer advice. He never gave one without the other; he was a believer in balance.

"Nice job on those flower beds, son. But let's keep an eye out for those grubs."

The worst job I ever had was picking up roadkill for the state highway department.

If I weren't a pastor, I would want to be a clerk for the library's information phone line. People call and ask you questions, such as what year George Washington was born (1732), or how many furlongs are in a mile (eight), or the capital of Finland (Helsinki). Dispensing valuable information is a worthwhile service, a blow against ignorance. Persons with this job can go home at night confident their work has made a difference.

The last time I called the information line was to learn the population of the United States. A man named Pat answered the phone. I asked him the question and listened as he paged through his world almanac. In 1996 our population was 265,563,000, he reported. Then he told me that by the year 2020 there'll be 323,052,000 of us. The United States has 3,615,292 square miles of land. That means, Pat informed me, there'll be 89.35709 of us per square mile. He sounded worried, but that doesn't seem crowded to me. I've seen that many folks crammed into the first three rows of an airplane.

I asked Pat what kind of people call the information line. All kinds, he said, but mostly people in bars. Friday nights are his busiest time. People in bars bet on trivia, such as the atomic number of oxygen. I guess alcohol harkens them back to high school chemistry. Atomic number of oxygen...hmm...is it eight or ten? Bets are placed. They call Pat. Eight, he tells them. Cheers and groans are heard in the background. Our tax dollars hard at work.

This information line is a service my hometown library never provided. "Look it up yourself," I was told. That's what happens when you combine library science with rugged individualism and the Protestant work ethic. "Look it up yourself. Can't you read? Who do you think I am, your servant?" A mammoth dictionary, its pages worn and tattered, rested on a stand next to the encyclopedias. Between the two a person could unlock the mysteries of the universe.

Mrs. Cox was our librarian. Ordinarily a gentle woman, she battled literary sloth with a vengeance. We met when I was eight years old and began visiting the library every Saturday. I wanted to read about cars, but Mrs. Cox steered me toward the biographies. "If you're going to read, read about great people," she told me. She handed me a book about Helen Keller and about how Miss Sullivan taught her to read by tracing the word "water" on her hand while standing at the pump in the Kellers' yard. Today you can go to Helen Keller's house and see the very pump where Helen Keller got her start with knowledge.

Knowledge is a wonderful thing, whether traced in your hand pumpside or dispensed over the information line. The Pats and Mrs. Coxes of the world do a noble work. Still, knowledge has its downside. The writer of Ecclesiastes cautioned that too much knowledge is a vexation, that he who increases knowledge increases sorrow. I don't understand that entirely, but I think it has to do with our tendency to regard human wisdom as our salvation. Living as we do on the heels of the

Holocaust and Hiroshima ought to be enough to remind us that knowledge misapplied can breed the deepest pain.

Great people not only fill their heads, they fill their hearts; they remember that what we do is every bit as important as what we know. My old boss Louie never went to college and died an unlettered man, but the lessons he taught are with me still. I was blessed that during the season of my book-learning years, I had Louie in the summertime, a man whose life lessons filled in the cracks my book lessons failed to cover.

The fruit of the Spirit
is love, joy, peace,
patience, kindness,
goodness, faithfulness . . .

The
Unclouded Day

*E*very time we visit my mother-in-law, Ruby,
we take a drive through the country. One
Saturday morning we drove down
Marengo Road.

"There's Dottie's Beauty Salon," Ruby
pointed out.

Dottie's Beauty Salon is owned by Dottie Barton, who married Oscar Barton when he got back
from the war in '45. Oscar went to work at the
chair factory in Paoli. Dottie went to beautician's
college in Louisville and got a license to cut hair.

She set up shop in her basement. Three hair
dryers along one wall, a chair in the middle where
Dottie works her magic, and another row of chairs
where the ladies wait their turn. A few *Good
Housekeeping* magazines, a coffeepot in the corner
with a help-yourself sign, and a little piece of cardboard on the wall that reads *Haircuts—$3.00*,
which is what she charges to this day. Three dollars. Dottie doesn't want to price herself out of

business, so she makes her living down in the basement three dollars at a time.

Oscar worked in town at the chair factory on a lathe, turning chair legs. He'd come home at night with sawdust in his ears, sit in his easy chair, and smoke his pipe. He and Dottie would talk about their day and watch *Jeopardy!* One night Oscar started coughing. After a couple of nights of that, Dottie said, "Honey, you'd better have that looked at."

So Oscar went to the doctor, who ran some tests and told him it was cancer. Too much sawdust and pipe tobacco.

The doctor gave him six months. Oscar took leave from the chair factory and sat at home in his easy chair, watching TV. Dottie would run up from the basement between haircuts to check on him or fluff his pillow or change the channel.

One day when she had two customers under hair dryers, one in the chair, and three waiting in the bull pen, Dottie ran upstairs and found Oscar dead. She sat beside him for a while, patting his hand and remembering back to 1945. Then she rose to her feet and went back downstairs.

The women asked, "How's Oscar?"

Dottie said, "He's gone."

They gathered around her, consoling her. "Maybe you ought to call the sheriff," they told her.

Dottie said, "No, not yet. I need to finish cutting your hair."

They thought to themselves, *Well, we're going to a funeral. We might as well look nice.*

So Dottie cut their hair. Two hours later she called the sheriff, and three days after that she was singing "Unclouded Day" at the funeral home in Paoli.

People still talk about it down there, about Dottie Barton and how when life knocked her to the ground, she rose to her feet, brushed herself off, and kept right on cutting hair.

She reminds me of Ruth. Ruth was a woman in the Bible who fell in love with a foreigner. They married, but he died before they could have any children. Left Ruth with a whole host of obligations, not the least of which was caring for his widowed mother, Naomi. Somewhere along the way, Ruth had learned about faithfulness, about how sometimes you have to chip away at burdens until they become blessings.

So when Naomi moved back home, Ruth went along. She told her mother-in-law, "Where you lay your head, I'll lay my head." They moved to Judah, where Ruth remarried and became the great-grandmother of King David. It really happened, just that way. Ruth kept going until burden became blessing, the same as Dottie.

That's what faithfulness does. It rises to its feet and

looks to the future, to the unclouded day. And it sings
of a home far away.

Inheritance Day

*I*n the autumn of my grandfather's ninety-second year, he moved to a retirement home. The decision to move had been a long time in the making. Grandma had died two years earlier. He was afraid that closing the door to their home one last time would make their good-bye permanent. Complicating the decision was their dog, Babe, who was going with him no matter what. Dispensing the family heirlooms was the final hurdle—the kitchen table he'd built from a wind-shook cherry tree in 1941, Grandma's mahogany bed, and the woodworking tools.

Since childhood, I had shown a penchant for tools of all types. I spent a fair portion of my youth perched on Grandpa's workshop stool, eyeing his implements and learning about their upkeep.

"Delta-Milwaukee drill press, built in 1939," he instructed. "Oil it once a month. Craftsman table saw. Don't ever buy a new one; just buy another motor when the old one goes bad. These are carving knives. Keep them sharp. A dull knife is a dangerous knife."

Then the most beautiful words of all to my young ears: "Someday these tools will be yours."

I could scarcely wait for them to be mine, not thinking how receiving them would signal Grandpa's final days. Whenever I visited him, I would finger the tools, imagining them in my workshop. But as I grew older and my affection for Grandpa increased, my yearning for his tools diminished. I began to realize they would be bought at a heavy price.

A week before he entered the retirement home, he invited me to his house. "Bring a truck," he said. I arrived the next morning with my friend Jim. Grandpa hobbled out to his workshop, and I followed. Jim had the good sense to linger in the background. Grandpa unlatched the door and we made our way inside.

He rested his hand on the drill press. "This is a 1939 Delta-Milwaukee drill press," he told me. "You'll need to oil it once a month." He worked his way through to the carving knives. "Remember to keep these sharp. A dull knife is a dangerous knife."

It was a sober morning.

My wife and I unloaded the tools that evening and carried them to my basement workshop. I arranged them just so while my little boy Spencer looked on from his perch on the workshop stool.

"This was Grandpa's drill press," I told him. "Now it belongs to me. And these are carving knives. When you're bigger I'll show you how to use them."

He looked up at me from the stool. "Can I have them?"

"Yes, Spencer, someday a long time from now, when Daddy doesn't need them anymore, these tools will be yours."

He grinned a shy grin. Those were beautiful words to his young ears.

Forty-five years from now, I'll totter out to my workshop with son in tow. It will be his Inheritance Day. I will have oiled the drill press once a month, just as Grandpa taught me to do. It will be one hundred years old and will work just fine. My son's friend will linger in the background, while Spencer and I go over the tools' upkeep one last time. "Don't forget, son, a dull knife is a dangerous knife."

I wonder if on that day my son will feel the melancholy I felt on my Inheritance Day. I wonder if he'll lie awake on that distant night, wishing his daddy was still long for this world, as I wish that now of Grandpa.

Late at night, when my sons are asleep and my wife is reading in her chair, I go down to my workshop and think of grandpas and daddies and sons and the faithful rhythm of it all.

The Heist

I live in the city. If you live in a small town, you probably already feel sorry for me. Pastoring a church in the city was not my idea; it was God's. God gets blamed for a lot of things. Some people blame God when they get sick. Others blame God if their marriages fail. I blame God for the theft of our CD player. If God had kept us at a country church, this would not have happened.

I installed the CD player in the car prior to a 2000-mile drive. My wife had vetoed the idea of a CD player the year before. So one week before our trip, I had the CD player secretly installed as a gift to her. I often pick out things I want and give them to her as gifts. Once for her birthday I gave her a set of wood chisels.

The CD player was stolen while the car sat in our driveway. I called our insurance man to report the theft. He was sympathetic and promised to send me the necessary paperwork to file a claim. Three days later, Charles the mailman delivered a six-page questionnaire. The first question asked where the car was when the theft occurred. I wrote that it was in our driveway. Why was the vehicle there, the next question asked. Because our garage is full of junk, I answered. Insurance companies are awfully nosy these days.

Another question asked for the police case number. I didn't have one of those. Bill hadn't given me one. Bill is our neighborhood policeman and lives down the street from us. He works the night shift, which is the only shift our neighborhood police department works. During the daylight hours, we fend for ourselves.

Bill sleeps until supper, so I waited until he was up and about before walking down to his house to give him the news. He was embarrassed. The year before, someone else had a CD player stolen from his car. Our neighborhood was enduring a crime wave, and Bill was taking it personally.

Bill asked if I had locked the car. Of course not, I told him. If I had locked the car, the thief would have broken out a window. Better to let him at it, I say. Bill agreed. Then he suggested I put lightbulbs in my security lights. I had unscrewed the lightbulbs because they attract bats. I was afraid the bats would get tangled in my hair and drive me mad. Bill suggested I buy a hat. These are the hidden costs of crime we never think about.

Later that night, I was going through the house, turning off lights and drawing the blinds. I looked out the window. A man was walking down our lane. He stopped at our bushes and crouched there a long time. I continued to watch him. When my eyes adjusted to the darkness, I could see it was Bill. He was on a stakeout. It was cold and rainy. I wanted to take him coffee, but I had the feeling he didn't want anyone to know he was there.

I talked with him the next day. He mentioned he had been down to our house the night before. No luck, he said, but he promised to keep a close eye on things. He said sometimes a thief will give folks a week or two to replace a stolen CD player, then come back and steal the new one. So Bill has been keeping watch. I see him while I'm drawing the blinds, crouched in the bushes, his hat pulled down to keep out the bats.

If he manages to get by Bill, the thief will be in for a surprise. We didn't buy a new CD player. Instead, we took the insurance money and bought my wife a dulcimer. After the kids are asleep, Joan sits in the front room and plays. Every half hour, Bill drives down the lane and looks things over.

A long while back, the psalmist wrote about a God who neither slumbers nor sleeps, about a God who stands watch all night long, who keeps us from evil and evil from us. A celestial Bill.

I lie in bed and think of God and Bill keeping faithful watch as echoes of a dulcimer hang in the air. Fear can keep us up all night long, but faith makes one fine pillow.

The
Open Door

*I*n 1948 a tornado ripped through our town and leveled Saint Mary's Catholic Church, where my family worshiped. It was the only church destroyed in town, which caused some of our town's more doctrinaire Protestants to speculate that God's judgment might somehow have been involved. This was back in the days before ecumenism and tolerance. When my Baptist father married my Catholic mother, families on both sides were aghast. My great-uncle warned my father of the Catholic conspiracy to wed Baptists, bear their children, and give the kids to the pope. I'm certain there were days when my father prayed mightily for the pope to take us away.

This ecclesiastical crisis was resolved when my father elected to dispense with religion altogether and stay home to read the Sunday paper. Mom rousted us out of bed and marched us over to the Catholic church. Saint Mary's didn't have a nursery as churches do now, so we kids would squeeze into a pew next to Mom. Five against one. My sainted mother would kneel to pray, clasp her hands, and close her eyes. We children would sag in the pew, envying our pagan neighbors.

One Sunday morning as my mother was deep in prayer, I slipped from the pew, went next door to Pleas Lilly's gas station, and spent my offering money on penny candy. I made it back just in time for Father McLaughlin's sermon, which was about a husband and wife who had lied to the church and spent their offering money on themselves. When they walked into the church, God struck them dead. As I was listening, the Tootsie Rolls congealed in my stomach, an immovable mass, a testament to sin and disobedience. I fell to my knees beside my mother, endeavoring to pray my sorry soul out of perdition. Though I have prayed many times since that day, I can't recall another time I beseeched the Lord with such passion.

Later that afternoon, I confided my sin to my brother Glenn, who pointed out that God often waits to smite us until we are sleeping. This, he explained, is why the devil never sleeps. This seemed consistent with what I already knew to be true; I had once heard a TV preacher thunder that the devil never slept. And that night, neither did I. I lay awake repeating over and over again the phrase "I love Jesus. I love Jesus. I love Jesus," hoping God would think twice before killing someone with such sweet praise on his lips.

When morning dawned, I prized the tender mercies of God as never before. And I have, since that time, believed with all my being that were I to stray from God's house to sin, the pathway home would lead always to an open door. Such deep consolation does faith provide.

This gospel of the open door in no way originated with me. Jesus once told of a son who had wandered away to sin and returned home to love, of one whose self-trust turned to father-trust. "I will arise, and I will return to my father," said the prodigal.

And the son arose and walked homeward toward a father

...whose eyes were peeled for a son's return,

...who kept a robe pressed and ready,

...who had the family ring shined and polished, and

...who had the homecoming meal at oven's door.

Such deep consolation does faith provide.

Now this I tell to all who have wandered far away. That even now God searches the road, awaiting your return. That it's never too late to turn homeward. Your robe is pressed, and your ring is polished; for your finger it was made. The meal is on; your chair awaits. And our God of the open door stands waiting, yearning to herald your return. "Yes, here he is. I see him now. Bring the robe. My child is home."

Dreamers All

There's a little town in northern Indiana named New London. It was founded over 150 years ago by Quakers from North Carolina who had made themselves a nuisance by helping slaves escape to freedom.

Their neighbors had told them, "Why don't you move to Indiana? We hear there's plenty of cheap land up there."

That's how we Quakers ended up in Indiana—because of a conscience that could not abide slavery and because we like a bargain. We're not only moral; we're practical.

The people who established New London had high aspirations. They founded that little town on the Indiana prairie, expecting it might one day dwarf its Old World namesake. They built a log meetinghouse in 1847 and petitioned to become the county seat, but that honor fell to Kokomo, ten miles to the east. Still, New London grew. It had its own doctor, a dozen stores, a couple hundred households, and a Quaker academy. When farmers went to town, New London was where they went.

The town grew bigger, and in 1856 the Quakers built a wood-frame meetinghouse that held a thousand people. The Civil War came. Quakers with a two-hundred-year history of pacifism took up arms and marched south. At war's end they came home, stained by the world. They asked the Lord to forgive their warring ways. The New London meetinghouse echoed with sobs of penance.

Then they settled in and raised families. But sons and grandsons raised on the farm traded in their plows for jobs in Kokomo. In 1905, the Quakers built a smaller meetinghouse. The New London Quaker Academy became the New London Public School. The doctor died, and the farmers started trading in Russiaville, two miles down the road. Houses burned down and were never rebuilt. Stores were shuttered. In 1951, the Quaker meetinghouse burned to the ground. A new meetinghouse was built, this time from stone.

My friend Ann pastors the New London Friends Meeting. A meeting that once drew a thousand now pulls in forty or fifty people. Ann is not discouraged. "Someday people are going to get tired of all those smokestacks in Kokomo, and when they do they'll move out here to New London," she says. She arrives early every Sunday morning and throws open the doors, ready for their return.

Ann is from the drill sergeant school of theology. She wants to keep her congregation fit and ready to minister to all the people who'll be attending their Quaker meeting just as soon as they come to their senses. Her congregation is an older one. She's concerned they'll be too frail to minister. So two years ago, she started them on an exercise program. Three times a week she unlocks the meetinghouse doors, turns on the lights, and powers up the organ. The New London Quakers straggle in. Ann plays the organ while they march in circles around the meetinghouse benches. She plays music to march by: "Stepping in the Light," "Just a Closer Walk with Thee," "It Is Glory Just to Walk with Him," and "I Never Walk Alone." They walk for an hour, then turn off the lights, lock the doors, and go visit their neighbors to invite them to Sunday worship.

Most every January, I drive north to New London on a Monday evening. We sit around a table in the meetinghouse basement and talk about their goals for the upcoming year. They are an ambitious people. It's in their blood. I ask them what they want to do that year.

"Convert the whole town," they answer. "All fifty families. We'll start with the children." They plan picnics and vacation Bible schools. I worry that their plans are too grand and want to caution them against unreasonable expectations. Then I figure if you're going to dream, you might as well go for broke.

"What do you want to do after you convert New London?" I ask them.

"Convert Kokomo," they tell me. More than 46,000 people in that smoky metropolis, but those forty Quakers aren't discouraged.

We close the meeting by praying for each family in town. They travel up and down the streets in their minds, praying for each household. It doesn't take long since there are only two streets. We break up for the night. The next day is marching day.

"See you tomorrow morning," Ann tells them. "Remember to wear comfortable shoes."

I know God will reward their faithfulness, though maybe not in their lifetimes. They are akin to Moses, who spied the Promised Land from afar without living to enjoy it. True for many of us who march unceasingly for a prize we'll never claim this side of heaven. That's what faith is: the assurance of things hoped for, the conviction of things not seen.

Sunday morning at New London Friends Meeting. "We're on day one of our seven-day Jericho," Ann reminds them. "But don't forget: We never walk alone. Now let's pray for our town."

One hundred and fifty years of faithful prayers and dreams. As the people pray, I imagine those old Quakers buried out back lifting their sainted hands and praying right along. Dreamers all.

The fruit of the Spirit
is love, joy, peace,
patience, kindness,
goodness, faithfulness,
gentleness. . .

Fussing, Fighting, and Forgiving

A friend of mine was fired from his job a while back. He came to tell me about it. He was embarrassed and didn't want to use the word "fired," but that's what had happened. He'd made his boss mad and had been fired. He was discouraged. I told him not to worry about it, that people get fired all the time and go on to better things.

I was fired from the first church I ever pastored. I had been there three months when an elderly woman asked a theological question about the end times. I told her my honest opinion, which must have been the wrong thing to do, because the next Sunday they held a meeting to talk about firing me. They told me if I changed my mind, I could keep my job. I asked them why they would want a pastor who surrendered his convictions just to keep his job. I started to resign but wasn't quick enough, and they fired me.

That very afternoon I got a phone call from another church to be their pastor. The next Sunday

I went to preach a trial sermon. I didn't want to be their pastor because they were a fundamentalist church and I didn't want to get fired again when they found out what I thought about the end times. So I preached a liberal sermon in hopes they wouldn't hire me. The congregation sat in the pews and squirmed. Except for one dear, sweet, elderly woman who smiled broadly and said, "Amen!" I found out later she was hard of hearing.

After worship, they tromped downstairs to talk about whether they should hire me. I sat upstairs in the meeting room and listened through the heating vent. Their initial comments were not promising. I was grateful my mother wasn't there to hear what they were saying about me. But then someone mentioned how maybe God had sent me their way so I could learn a little something. They quieted down and thought about that for a while. Then a man named Dick said, "I think we ought to hire him." Dick had moved to the country after his retirement. He was a big man who brooked no nonsense.

A few minutes later, I heard Dick tramp up the stairs. He sat down on the pew beside me. "We've reached agreement," he reported. "We've agreed that none of us liked your sermon. We've also agreed to call you to be our pastor."

I went out to the car, where my wife was waiting. "How did it go?" she asked me.

"Bad news," I told her. "They hired me."

That afternoon the phone rang. It was Dick, asking me if I would play golf with him. I was a little put out with him since he had criticized my sermon. I figured I could pay him back by thrashing him in a game of golf. We met the next morning at the golf course and played nine holes. Dick beat me by ten strokes. Afterward, when he was loading my clubs into the trunk of his car, he shook his head and laughed, "A preacher who can't preach or golf. What have we gotten ourselves into?"

Then he took me back to his house for lunch. I met his wife, Katie, a tender, considerate woman. "Heard about your sermon," she said. She was too polite to tell me what she'd heard about it.

Dick and I became fast friends. When I preached a sermon he didn't like, I was always the first to know. We golfed once a month. I never beat him. Then his elderly mother died, and I conducted her funeral. It was about then that Dick started liking my sermons. I never did figure out if it was because I was changing or because Dick was.

I stayed in that little church for four years. When I left, they gave me a book full of letters about what I meant to them. I sat downstairs in the meetinghouse basement and read it and cried. Wonderful, wonderful, wonderful people.

The next year I was at the hospital, visiting some-one in my new church. I saw Dick walking down the hall. He was crying. His Katie had died. Dick asked me if I could give her funeral, just as I'd said words over his mother. I have a rule about not going back to a former church to do funerals or weddings, but I couldn't bring myself to tell Dick no. Five years before, he'd taken a chance on me, and I figured that put me in his debt.

A couple of years later, I got a phone call from a lady in my old church. She told me Dick had cancer. By then I had children and a busier life. I went by to see Dick once, but he wasn't there. He died a few months later, before I could see him again to tell him how much he'd meant to me. His sons asked me to conduct his funeral. I broke my rule again and agreed to do it.

At the funeral I talked with some folks about how Christians these days can't seem to get along. How we fuss and fight and draw our theological lines in the sand. I told them how Dick and I were poles apart sometimes, but we'd made up our minds that dis-agreeing about God would never keep us from loving God's children. It's good to know where you stand, but it's even better to have your heart turned toward gentleness.

Dick ended up changing me in ways I needed to

be changed. I'd like to think I did the same for him. Maybe that's what God has in mind when he brings different folks together—that we each bring our scraps of truth and piece them together into this radiant quilt that is so much finer than anything we could have ever made alone.

If I hadn't been fired, I might never have learned that.

The Admonition Suit

One of the benefits of pastoring a small church is that you don't have to dress up. Most days I wear blue jeans, except on Sundays when I wear khakis and a sport coat. In the summer I wear short-sleeved shirts. A friend bought me a tie that has a picture of dogs playing poker on it. When I wear that, I have to sneak it out of the house and tie it on in the meetinghouse restroom. Otherwise, Joan won't let me out of the house.

I have one suit. It's charcoal gray with a suggestion of plaid. It looks like something you would wear to a funeral, which is the reason I bought it. That, and it was on sale for half price. I also wear it to weddings. On the rare occasion a fancy church invites me to speak, I wear it then, too. I have it cleaned once a year, which tells you how much I wear it.

One Sunday morning I was getting dressed for meeting. All my khakis were in the laundry basket. I had bought three identical pairs at the same time, on sale, and they were all dirty. Some of the men in our Quaker meeting wear blue jeans to church, but I didn't think I could get away with that. That left my suit, so I put it on, hid the dog tie in my pocket, and walked across the parking lot to the meetinghouse.

I stood at the meetinghouse door, greeting people. We have a number of vigorous hand-shakers and huggers in our meeting, so people would pump my hand, hug me, then comment on my suit. I explained that my khakis were dirty.

One of our members, Alice, is a dear ninety-one-year-old whose father had been a Quaker pastor. She liked that I was wearing a suit. Except for the dog tie, it reminded her of her father. "You look like a preacher today," she said. I think a great deal of Alice and was pleased to make her happy.

Harold is one of my best friends. He came up the walk, saw me in my suit, and said, "Uh-oh."

"What do you mean 'Uh-oh'?" I asked.

"You're wearing your admonition suit," Harold said. "Every time you wear a suit, we end up getting preached at."

That bothered me. It's a common perception that pastors are often angry about something. I can see why people think that. Once I watched a preacher on television with the sound turned off. It looked like he was yelling the whole time. So I try to project an image of a caring, gentle pastor. I even volunteer in the church nursery once a year. Now Harold was talking about my admonition suit.

The next month I wore my suit again. Harold grinned when he saw it but didn't say anything. When I rose to preach, I looked directly at him as I spoke. Harold fidgeted in his seat, waiting for the wrath of God to erupt. Instead, I talked about God's love. By the time I was finished speaking, Harold was exhausted. The anticipation of wrath had drained him of strength.

Despite his wisecracks about my suit, Harold is a soft touch, one of those rare souls who leave you feeling like royalty. When some people treat you that way, it's because they want you to buy something. Harold has nothing to sell.

Harold is the most forthright person I know. A lot of times we confuse gentleness with blandness. Harold is anything but bland. If he disagrees with you, he says so, but he does it so matter-of-factly it is disarming. You end up not minding one bit that Harold disagreed with you. When some people disagree with me, I try to change their minds. When Harold disagrees with me, I rethink my position.

Most of us borrow the opinions of others without much critical thought. Harold thinks a lot. I suspect that's what makes him gentle. True gentleness is grounded in knowledge. I think God is gentle because he knows us so well. It's easier to be gentle with people when you know their hurts.

When I first met Harold, he told me that he had grown up all over the world because his dad was in the military. Harold had been in the military too. I remember thinking that maybe God had brought us together so I could teach Harold what it meant to be a gentle, peace-loving Christian. That was four years ago. I've learned a lot since then.

I spend every Thursday evening with Harold and four other men. We sit around and read about the saints of old—Augustine and Luther and Calvin. I wonder if four hundred years from now folks will be studying Harold.

Dump Boy

When I was nine, my parents bought a house on the south edge of town on the road to the landfill. A family's station in life could be measured by its proximity to the dump. We were solid middle class and therefore lived beyond most of the dump's stench. Two or three days a month we could smell it, just enough to remind us that we were rich enough to avoid the smell most of the time but not wealthy enough to escape it altogether.

Down the road from us, dumpward, lived an old woman and two children. No man. Just that woman and those two kids in a dirty white house down a long, gravel thread of a lane. Where house ended and dump began was barely discernible.

The boy would walk up the road to play with us. When children play, a natural pecking order evolves—an overdog and an underdog. He was the underdog, and we overdogs pointed our barbed arrows of meanness his way. He responded as a cornered dog would, with snarls and bites and lunges, which served to confirm our judgment of him—wild kid, out of control, dump boy.

When things heated up, powerful and potent weapons were unsheathed: "You better leave me alone, or my dad will get you!" This was a weapon he seemed unable to counter. No elevated retort, no "Oh, yeah? Well I'll get my dad, and he'll beat up your dad!" Just silence, a turning away, and a walking dumpward.

I don't remember now how the knowledge came to us, but come to us it did—that his father and mother had been killed and the old woman in the dirty white house was his grandma. I do remember that it had no effect on us; the meanness continued. Despite popular thinking, gentleness is not something we are born with; it is something we are taught, and we had not yet learned it.

The lesson came during a basketball game when an elbow was thrown and dump boy charged my brother . . . fists flying, rage brimming, right at my brother, who lifted not a hand to defend himself. My brother, who just the week before had chased dump boy back home and hurled rocks, now stood stone-still while dump boy battered him. It was an unleashing of fury such as I had never seen, dump boy lashing out at every pain that had ever come his way: the midnight visit of a sheriff's chaplain who explained that Mommy and Daddy wouldn't be coming home, the taunts of children who punished him for his grandma's house, the arrows of meanness which pierce the air and then the soul. Fury raining down.

"Hit him, hit him!" we yelled at my brother. But he raised not a hand, and after a time dump boy tired of the easy kill and went home. We assailed my brother with questions, demanding an explanation for his timidity in battle. He mumbled something about not being able to hit a boy who had lost his parents, that he'd been hit enough as it was.

I did not understand then. And still I struggle with its meaning—how gentleness is never real until fury is aimed our way, how I can be gentle with my infant son but think ill of the eight-item man in the seven-item line at the grocery store. Such little acts turn our hearts from gentleness.

Jesus knew this, knew it not only in his head, but in his heart—that gentleness, of all the fruits, is the hardest to cultivate. How strong our tendency to return the blow, to hurl the rock, to call the name. Until our hearts are likewise broken. Why is it that gentleness must necessarily spring from rocky soil, from hardship, from ground sowed with tears?

One day, I prayed to the Lord to teach me gentleness and sat about, waiting for good to happen. Instead, God showed me sorrow, and thus began my education.

Dump boy moved away the next year. I haven't seen him since. Don't even know if he's alive. I hope his life is sweet, that he married well, that tiny children crowd his lap and call him sweeter names than we did.

Rivers of Mercy

I met Lyman and Harriet when I interviewed to become the pastor of Irvington Friends Meeting. The whole meeting turned out to look me over. All twelve people. We sat around a table on folding chairs. Harriet had made snacks. Halfway into my first chocolate chip cookie, Lyman explained that the church was crippling along. He was a retired coach, accustomed to getting at the heart of the matter.

"We've got enough money to last two years; then we'll have to close 'er down," he told me. "You want to be our pastor?"

I chewed on the cookie, trying to decide if I wanted to hitch my wagon to this falling star. I looked at Harriet. She smiled and offered me another cookie. The chocolate chips were warm from the oven. When I bit into them, threads of chocolate draped across my lower lip.

"We have cookies at every meeting," Harriet said.

"I think the Lord is calling me here," I intoned,

plucking a crumb from my lap and popping it in my mouth. "Could you pass the cookies, please?"

So it was by virtue of Harriet's cookies that my wife and I settled in to the friendly environs of this little Quaker meeting.

After the interview, Lyman the coach shook my hand and clapped me on the back. "We can turn this church around if we all pitch in and work hard. It'll be a big job; it'll take a lot of teamwork; it'll take all of us working together."

I pumped his hand up and down. I couldn't wait to get started.

"Teamwork, yes. All of us working together, yes," I echoed.

"Oh, by the way," he said, "Harriet and I are going away for the summer."

They came back in the fall. On Halloween, Harriet baked dozens of cookies and we went door to door, passing them out to our neighbors as we invited them to church.

A few weeks later, a woman called our meeting. "Do you offer child care during worship?" she asked.

"We most certainly do," I answered, not letting on that we didn't have any children to care for.

I called Harriet on the phone. "We need a nursery before Sunday," I told her.

Harriet called Oneida and Dolores and Denise.

By Sunday our storage room was carpeted and freshly painted, and there were new curtains hanging at the windows. A toy chest sat in the corner, filled with dump trucks and dolls.

That Sunday, a woman and her baby daughter came to visit.

"Welcome to Irvington Friends," Harriet told them. "Would you like to see our nursery?"

That week the phone rang. It was a man calling to see if we had any children in our church. He didn't want his kids to be the only children here.

I told him the children here were keeping us hopping—a strong truth.

The next year we had enough children to start an evening program. Harriet helped cook the meal, and Lyman taught the class. Before the meal, he would gather the kids for a blessing. He would pray aloud, dropping hints about expected behavior. "Lord, we just pray the boys and girls here learn from their teachers. We pray they behave themselves and that you bless them. Amen." Then the kids would fall into line. Lyman always put the girls up front. "Ladies first," he told the boys.

That was on Wednesday evenings. On Mondays and Tuesdays, Lyman volunteered at a homeless shelter. He'd come to church on Sundays and announce the various needs at the shelter. One Sunday he talked about Mike. Mike was a young man the shelter had cut loose because they thought he was drunk. Lyman went to visit him in the abandoned building where he was living and befriended him. After several months and many trips to the doctor, they learned that Mike's stumbling wasn't due to alcohol, but to Huntington's chorea, a degenerative nerve disease. No cure, eventually fatal, a living hell of a sickness.

Lyman found Mike an apartment and filled it with furniture. Then he got Mike signed up for government disability. Every time I pay my taxes, I think of Mike in his little apartment. Mike, who shakes so badly he can't keep himself clean. What a fine use of our money, to help the Mikes of the world. Lyman would go to visit Mike three times a week, take him to the doctors, put clothes on his back, and do his shopping for him.

One Sunday during meeting for worship, Lyman reported that Mike was getting worse. He'd tried to melt marshmallows and shook so badly that the hot marshmallows had poured out on his hand, burning him to the bone. Mike needed to be somewhere with round-the-clock care, so Lyman was looking for a place to take him. He asked us to pray for Mike.

A few months later, Lyman and I were talking. I asked how Mike was doing.

"We've found a place for him," Lyman told me. There was no "we" about it. Lyman had spent nearly all of his waking hours finding a place for Mike and raising the money for his care, but when it came time to take credit, "I" became "we."

Lyman said they were going to move him the next Saturday.

"Mike needs a new bed," he told me. Saturday was my day off, and I didn't want to spend it moving Mike, so before Lyman could ask for my help, I told him my contribution would be to buy Mike a new bed. Lyman thanked me profusely, then wondered aloud if he'd be able to find enough people to help Mike move. I told him not to worry, that the Lord would provide. Sometimes when I say that, I really mean it. Other times I say the Lord will provide because I'm not going to. This was one of those times.

I saw Lyman the day before the move. He was smiling. He had been to the bank to give them Mike's new address. He was telling the bank manager how Mike had Huntington's chorea and couldn't take care of himself, so they were moving him to an apartment with supervised care but there weren't enough people to help him move, so Lyman had been praying to the Lord.

The banker looked at Lyman and said in a quiet voice, "My brother had Huntington's chorea. I'll help you move him."

Now angels of mercy attend Mike's every need.

Once a week, Lyman stops in to sit with him. Then he comes by to visit me. He plops himself down in the rocking chair in my office. If it's noon, we watch *The Andy Griffith Show*. When it's over, Lyman talks about how wonderful it would be if folks were as kind and gentle in real life as they are in Mayberry.

"Yeah, wouldn't that be wonderful?" I reply. We rock a little more back and forth, the coach and the pastor.

"Church is going well," Lyman says. "I don't think we'll have to close the doors. We have you to thank for that."

"It's not me," I tell him. "It's the Lord. He provides."

Lyman looks at me and grins. "Boy, isn't that the truth?" he says.

And rivers of mercy run over their banks.

Pam

A year after I became pastor of our little Quaker meeting, Jay began attending. He lived in the neighborhood and worked for the Department of Defense. I remember being excited at the prospect of converting him to our pacifist ways. Jay showed up because he'd met a Quaker while he was at college, and she'd made a good impression on him. Her name was Pam.

When their paths crossed a few years after college and they discovered each was romantically unencumbered, Jay and Pam began seeing one another. After a couple of months, Jay brought her to meeting for worship. I remember thinking how she seemed to be the kind of woman every decent man hopes to find—a proper blend of lace and backbone.

They were married on February 15, 1992. Pam moved into Jay's house, down the road and around the corner from us. Since they lived nearby, we gave them a meetinghouse key in case someone needed in. The next Sunday I came to church to find the chairs turned every which way. Some were facing the back; some were facing forward; others were turned toward the windows. There was a note on the pulpit that read, *The Seating Committee met but could not reach agreement.* It was in Jay's handwriting, but when I'd walked up to the meetinghouse that morning, I'd noticed two sets of footprints in the snow.

The next spring, when the wildflowers bloomed, Jay spoke in meeting for worship and said they were expecting a child in late October. The rest of us clapped and whistled. Quakers are ordinarily a reserved people, but in the face of good news, we can become as riotous as Baptists. Pam sat beside Jay, blushing furiously.

A few weeks later, my telephone rang. It was Pam. "Can you come to the house?" she asked.

Pam had been to the doctor that day for a pregnancy checkup. Tests were run. One came back unusual—a blood test counting her white blood cells. "It might be leukemia," the doctor told her. He said she'd have to come back the next day for more tests. Pam went home and called Jay, her family, and me. We gathered in her home and stood in a circle, holding hands, Pam's father being brave and her mother crying, dripping tiny ponds of sorrow on the hardwood floor as we prayed God's best for Pam.

The next day was when the doctor was supposed to tell us everything was fine, that an error had been made. Instead, he told Pam she might want to abort her baby so she could start her treatment for leukemia. She decided against that. Instead she said she was going to have her child, spend a year cuddling him, then begin her treatment. And that's precisely what she did. Christopher was born October 24, 1993. Pam would hold him and talk about how she was going to whip the leukemia and raise her son. Not one of us doubted her.

At the start of Christopher's second winter, Pam checked into the hospital. They dosed her with radiation to kill her bone marrow and transplanted new marrow back into her. She had to lie off by herself behind a clear plastic curtain. Her parents would bring Christopher to see her. They'd hold him up to the curtain, and Pam would reach through with gloves and squeeze his plump hand. Jay would take time from work and sit behind the curtain with her, masked and gowned and gloved. Every Sunday at meeting we prayed for her, and once a day someone from our church visited her. Her parents and sisters kept a vigil in the waiting room.

Success. The transplant took. Pam went home to hold Christopher; Jay went back to work. The next Sunday at meeting our thanks to God shook the rafters.

But our cheers soon faded. In her weakened state, Pam contracted a virus and ran a fever. They took her back to the hospital, back behind the plastic curtain. And she never left. In her final weeks, the doctors pulled aside the curtain and let us gather around—her husband, her parents, her sisters, her friends, her pastor, and some days her little boy with his plump hands and his one-tooth grin.

On June 8, 1995, Pamela Janney died. Five days later, we laid her to rest in the cemetery at Walnut Ridge Friends Meeting, just down the road from the farm where she was born. Her parents drive by her grave and remember when she was little and how they taught her not to cross the road without looking for cars, never dreaming that a virus would one day strike down their blond-haired baby girl.

The Department of Defense closed the base where Jay worked. He went back to college to get a degree so he could teach. Jay and Christopher come to meeting every Sunday. Chris has Pam's gentle smile and blond hair. He sits on Jay's lap during worship, with Jay hugging him close. When our youth minister, Martha, takes the kids out for their own special worship, she walks them past a little tree we planted in Pam's memory. Every spring it bursts forth with white flowers, and we marvel at its beauty. Just like we used to do when Pam was among us.

The fruit of the Spirit
is love, joy, peace,
patience, kindness,
goodness, faithfulness,
gentleness, and
self-control.

Getting Rid
of Things

A big problem we face today is the increasing difficulty of getting rid of things we neither need nor want. For years I've been trying to throw away one dozen half-empty paint cans. I tried setting them out with the trash, but the garbage man wouldn't take them. He said a half-empty paint can is considered toxic waste. They don't want it in a landfill, but it's all right down in my basement next to my children's playroom. I'm grateful our government is doing all it can to keep our dumps clean.

I have a farmer friend who wanted to get rid of an old toilet. The trash man wouldn't take it, either. My friend had just bought a new TV. He put the toilet in the TV box, loaded it in his truck, and drove to the shopping mall in the city. He went inside for half an hour, and when he came out, the TV box was gone and the toilet with it. I thought maybe I'd try that with my paint cans.

When I inherited my grandpa's woodworking bench, I had to get rid of my old bench. Once a month we have heavy-trash pickup in our neighborhood. Theoretically, you can set out any large item, and the trash man will haul it away. I dragged the workbench up out of the basement and carried it to the curb. I thought as long as it was heavy-trash pickup day, I'd set out some other things. When I came back to the curb with more junk, a woman was standing next to the workbench. She had a protective grasp on it, as if she was afraid someone would happen down the road and wrestle it from her.

"Are you going to take my workbench?" I asked.

"Sure am," she answered. "My husband's gone to fetch the truck."

"I have a table with a broken leg down in the basement. Would you like that, too?" I asked.

"We'll take anything," she said.

"Anything?" I asked. "Even paint?"

"Sure, we'll take paint."

I didn't tell her it was toxic waste.

Once you start getting rid of things, it's hard to stop. Lately we've had too many distant relatives and traveling preachers spending the night at our house. We got to thinking that if folks had to sleep on our couch, they'd stay home and sleep in their own beds. We called the Salvation Army, and they hauled away the furniture in our guest bedroom. I wish we'd thought of that ten years ago.

I had a bicycle that I had to ride all scrunched down. I didn't mind that when I was younger, but now it hurts my back. I tried for a year to get rid of that bike, but everyone I asked already had a bicycle. My brother finally agreed to take it off my hands for fifty dollars. I took the bike by his house and told him I'd pay him just as soon as I got the money.

The things I want most to be rid of are the hardest to dispose. For the past ten years, I've been the unhappy owner of a fiery temper. I am most likely to explode when faced with a household repair. I suspect some of these murder sprees we hear about on the news probably started with a leaky faucet. Whenever I have to fix something around the house, Joan takes the boys and doesn't come back until I'm finished yelling. This nasty little trait is not something I am proud of, and if I could find someone to take it off my hands, I would surrender it gladly. But nobody wants to take our faults from us. Everyone has enough of his own. It's just like bicycles.

When the apostle Paul wrote about the fruit of the Spirit, the last one he included was self-control. "Love, joy, peace, patience, kindness, goodness, faithfulness, gentleness, and, oh yes, one more: self-control." I do pretty well until that last one. I wish Paul had quit while I was ahead.

In the fifth chapter of Galatians Paul said that folks

who storm around mad won't inherit the kingdom of God. At the rate I'm going, the only thing I stand to inherit is Grandpa's workbench.

Lot of things I need to get rid of in my life, things that clutter my soul and squeeze out God. And I don't mean old paint and broken tables. I'm talking about anger so toxic it eats away at the soul. I'm grateful God has the last word in these matters, that he meets my failure with forgiveness, my temper with tenderness.

State Fair

*L*ast August our local paper showed a picture of the world's largest pig. New York boasts the Statue of Liberty; California, its Golden Gate Bridge; we Hoosiers extol our swine. *World's largest boar!* the headline trumpeted. The line to see the pig snaked through the pig barn and past the barbecue tent where folks were doing their best to match his weight. The pig lay on its side, so portly it couldn't support its bulk.

In that same newspaper was a story about a man who weighed so much he couldn't walk. The fire department had to lower him out a window. Even Richard Simmons tried to help him, but his family kept slipping him HoHos on the side. This happened in New York City, where a hefty portion of the world's more unusual people reside. The remainder can be found at the Indiana State Fair.

I am partial to the exhibition tent. Pitchmen set out their wares—miracle knives that saw bricks then slice tomatoes paper-thin, miracle cleaners that dissolve bathtub rust, miracle vitamins that leave you frisky. At the state fair exhibition tent, miracles are as common as flies. If you don't exercise some measure of self-control, you can spend all your money in the exhibition tent and not have enough left to buy an elephant ear.

A healthy young woman was peddling the vitamins. I listened as she offered testimony upon testimony. "B. W. of Des Moines weighed 300 pounds. After six months of Miracle Vitamins, she weighs a slim 120. J. G. of Rhode Island was in the nursing home for three years. She took Miracle Vitamins and is back home mowing her yard." Isn't that a powerful incentive to get better?

I asked the healthy young woman if she had a vitamin for persons with a receding hairline and a slight paunch. She handed me two bottles. Twenty dollars. The vitamins to grow hair have proven successful on laboratory mice, she told me. Though they didn't work for me, I'm keeping them in the event I ever meet up with a bald mouse. The paunch vitamins weren't any better. I took them for a month, and my pants were still hard to fasten. Then I reread the vitamin label where it said in tiny print, *We recommend eating in moderation and daily exercise.* That probably means elephant ears are out of the question.

For the past twenty years or so, the Agape Apostolic Full Faith Bible Church has pitched a tent on the fairway leading to the carnival sideshows. You walk down the fairway to see the nekkid-as-the-day-she-was-born two-headed lady, and a man steps from the tent, Bible in hand, saying, "Howdy, brother. Can you spare a moment for the Lord?" Before you know it, you're inside the tent discussing Paul's epistle to the Romans. That tent, being where it is, has kept many a lustful youth from going astray.

The highlight of the state fair is Band Day. This is when high school marching bands from across the state gather to compete. Teenagers who rolled out of bed at sunrise each summer day to practice their steps are now vying for a headline of their own. They take to the field, swinging their instruments in a long-memorized cadence. Out of uniform they are gangly and awkward; now they step with elegant precision, the embodiment of discipline.

We sit in the bleachers and watch them—we who are not so disciplined ourselves, elephant ears in hand, the calls of carnival pitchmen ringing in our ears. We who take shortcuts, who take vitamins instead of walks—we watch those teenagers and envy their discipline. In this parade of gluttony and fleshly excess that is the state fair, their measured control is cool refreshment.

There's a story in the Bible about a man named Esau, who in a fit of weakness handed over a lifelong gift to indulge a short-term craving. It is always easier to gratify the self than it is to control it. I know this first-hand. In the past year, I've added two inches to my waistline. Some men hide girlie magazines; I hide HoHos. My wife measures the window, then looks at me and shakes her head. New York City, here we come.

The Birdhouse

A friend of mine has a serene office with rocking chairs and windows on two sides that look out into woods. The windows have screens. In warm weather he opens the windows and listens to the birds. Once when I was visiting him, I noticed a weathered birdhouse hanging on his wall.

"Why do you have a birdhouse in your office?" I asked him.

"That was my grandfather's," he told me. Then he told me how it came to hang on his wall.

The story began in 1949 in a little southern Indiana town. It was a Sunday morning in early June. My friend's Aunt Betty had just graduated from high school. Betty and her family attended the Baptist church, where they were singing the opening hymn one Sunday when Betty noticed a handsome young man across the aisle. He was a traveling Baptist, passing through on business. She knew nothing about him, but by the third verse had fallen in love with his strong jaw. Two weeks later she went away with him, and they were married.

A year later the traveling Baptist left her, and Betty returned home with a baby girl. Her father went to the train station to pick them up and drive them home. Betty sobbed the whole way; her tears rained down on her baby.

Her daddy told her, "You're always welcome to stay with us. Your mother and I still love you. You know that, don't you?"

The next Sunday, he took Betty and his little granddaughter back to church, and when people whispered about them, he stood tall, daring anyone to look crossways at them. When the preacher talked against divorced people and pointed fingers, Betty's father reached over and put his arm around his daughter and drew her close.

"My grandfather was a wonderful man," my friend told me. "He took in his little granddaughter, and he loved her as his own."

From the first moment he saw her in his daughter's arms at the train station, he became a father to her. He taught her how to swim at Dewart Lake and how to swing a bat and pitch a ball so no one could hit it. Taught her the kind of things fathers teach their daughters.

Then he came down with cancer. He spent his last spring on the back porch. His granddaughter sat with him. He was sixty-five and she was twelve. He was wrapping things up; she was just getting started. They sat on the back porch and listened to the birds. He taught her their songs.

"That's a wren. Over there in the linden tree is a mockingbird. Oh, my, there's a bluebird on the fence row. You don't see them too often."

One day in early May, she said, "Grandpa, let's go to town and buy a birdhouse."

They walked down to Fleming's Hardware and bought a birdhouse shaped like a log cabin and hung it from the back porch eaves and watched a wren build her nest and hatch her young.

That birdhouse was the last thing he ever bought. He died a month later. Today it hangs in my friend's office. He looks at it and remembers how a man opened his arms to a hurting daughter and her little baby, how he went to church and stood tall in the face of gossip and drew his daughter close when the stares grew hard. He died when my friend was one year old. He doesn't remember anything about his grandfather. All that he has from him is one birdhouse and the stories others tell about him.

His Aunt Betty remarried. She is seventy years old now and an elder in that same Baptist church, the first female elder they've ever had. Whenever young people in the church divorce, she ministers to them. She visits them in their homes and tells them, "We still love you. You know that, don't you?" She takes them back to church, and if other people look hard at them, she stands tall and puts her arm around them and draws them close.

One time the preacher got to talking about divorce and naming names. The next day Betty paid him a visit in his office and told him a little story about a young woman fresh out of high school in 1949, who fell in love with a young man and went away to get married, and how, to her deep shame and sorrow, it didn't work out. She's felt guilty about it ever since. People still talk about it. "Maybe," she told the preacher, "instead of pointing fingers, you can encourage these young people who have had their lives torn apart. Maybe you can help them put their homes back in order instead of pointing out the disrepair." The preacher listened and learned.

I listened to this story on an early summer day while sitting in my friend's office. The windows were open. A woodpecker beat a staccato rhythm high in a beech tree. My friend identified the bird, plucking its genus from somewhere deep in his genes. Yet another gift from his grandfather.

I rocked back and forth and thought on the vagaries of self-control, and how it is that God redeems even a hasty decision made back in 1949. I considered how God has salvaged my many failures, how God has met me at my places of shame, how he's drawn me close and helped me stand tall. One more Father doing the best he can by his child.

Flowers
and Weeds

Once a year my wife has a birthday. It's been that way as long as I've known her. Every year it's the same problem—what do you get the woman who has everything? Most of the time I buy her jewelry. One time I gave her a bracelet. She told me it was so beautiful she'd hate to lose it. So she put it in her jewelry box, where it's been ever since. It's still in perfect condition. She's taken fine care of it.

I decided one year to give her something she could use. Our iron was making funny noises on the steam setting, so I thought I would buy her a new iron. I asked my sister her opinion. She told me not to buy Joan an iron, that it wasn't very romantic. I'm glad I listened to my sister. Irons aren't very romantic. It would be like giving someone a vacuum cleaner. The boys and I went to Furrow's Hardware and bought her a wheelbarrow instead.

The week before, Joan and the boys had been outside cleaning up the yard, picking up sticks and putting them in the wheelbarrow. The load was unbalanced, and the wheelbarrow kept tipping over whenever Joan pushed it. So I bought her a wheelbarrow with two wheels. I don't mean to boast, but that kind of thoughtful consideration has enabled our marriage to flourish.

Whenever Joan works in the yard, she takes the boys with her. She's teaching them the difference between weeds and flowers. They're not in school yet, but they can already distinguish between wild bloodwort and shepherd's purse. Joan wants them to know these things before they're turned loose to hoe the flower beds. Though it isn't an easy lesson to teach, it's an important one to learn. Otherwise, they'll spend their lives confusing weeds for flowers and flowers for weeds.

Buying my wife a new wheelbarrow raised the problem of what to do with the old one. The tire had a slow leak. Every time we used it, we had to pump up the tire. If we used it more than an hour, we had to put more air in it. It's been like that all ten years we've owned it, a burden from day one. I filled the tire, hosed off the wheelbarrow, hung a *Free* sign on it, and hauled it to the curb.

A man down the street spied it, shiny and red, glistening in the sun, tire full. He wheeled it across the street to his yard, delighted with his unexpected find. I drove by his house later that day. He was pushing the wheelbarrow across his yard. It was full of sticks; the tire was flat. It tipped over and the sticks fell out. He began kicking the wheelbarrow. I could hear him cuss and swear. Ordinarily, he is a saintly man, but that wheelbarrow has tarnished many a halo.

This man has been living under a burden since the day he took up with that wheelbarrow. One falling domino after another. Because he didn't pick up the sticks, he rolled over a limb and broke his mower. While he was shopping for a new one, the dandelions moved in and took over. He ended up having to spray his entire yard. I was going to offer my help, but by then he wasn't speaking to me. All of this from a wheelbarrow marked *Free*.

We take some things into our lives which have a veneer of blessing, and they exact a price we can scarcely imagine. We confuse bane for blessing and blessing for bane. I watch Joan teach our sons the difference between flower and weed. I hope it will be a primer for their later years, that those garden lessons will be their start in lives of wise discernment. I hope they'll learn that just because something's sitting at the curb marked *Free*, doesn't mean it really is.

Jesus once taught about how the cares of the world can grind a plant down to nothing. These "cares" are the things we bring into our lives with scarcely a thought. They promise good and deliver ill—the material goods that enslave us, the relationships that crush our spirits, the careers that tax our souls. Most all of us have a flat-tired wheelbarrow haunting us one way or another. It helps to learn the difference between weeds and flowers, whether something should be left sitting at the curb or carried home with joy.

Leverne

When I was sixteen years old, I bought my first motorcycle. It was lime green and crept down the road at thirty miles an hour. It was tiny and I was tall, which gave the appearance of a praying mantis on wheels. The next year I sold it and bought a bigger motorcycle. It went sixty miles an hour, but only downhill with a stiff wind at my back.

I rode that motorcycle for two years, then sold it and bought an even bigger one. The speedometer went up to a hundred, but the fastest I ever went was sixty-five. I rode it for three months, then my best friend, Tim, was killed on his motorcycle, so I sold mine.

Ten years later, my wife came home from work and announced, "Frank is selling his bike." Frank was a man she worked with. He had bought a motorcycle years before but seldom rode it. That night Joan and I went for a drive in the car.

"Let's go by Frank's house and see his motorcycle," I suggested.

The bike was sitting in his front yard. Blue and shiny and showroom pretty. I straddled it. Frank came out of his house. "Five hundred dollars," he whispered in my ear. That was exactly how much we had in our savings account. God's will was obvious. I rode the bike home that night.

This was before we had children. We'd come home from work and take rides deep into the country. On Friday nights we'd motor to my mother-in-law's farm two hours south, saddlebags crammed full, meandering along back roads, stretching the journey to three and four hours. My mother despised that bike, threatening to unleash a hammer on it. She called it the death machine.

My sister is a nurse. She regularly phoned to describe motorcycle riders who came to the hospital broken and mangled. But that motorcycle's lure was so strong, I could not help myself. When the work was done and the sun was out, I would ride and ride and ride.

After we had children, Joan stopped riding. She told me she didn't want the kids to be orphaned. I put the motorcycle up for sale and went bikeless. I bought a bicycle and pedaled around the neighborhood. It wasn't the same. By fall, I was depressed. I went to see Leverne, a therapist. I'd never been to a therapist before and was embarrassed at the prospect. I sat in her office and listened as she talked about the importance of maintaining balance in one's life.

"Too much work isn't good for people. We need outlets. We need to play," Leverne counseled.

The next day I bought a motorcycle, blue and shiny and showroom pretty. I pulled up in the driveway.

"I didn't want to," I told Joan, "but my therapist made me."

I named the motorcycle Leverne, my way of honoring the saint who'd delivered me from the clutches of depression.

Leverne sat in the garage all winter. I added a windshield, put more chrome on her, changed her oil, and fitted her with saddlebags. On a March morning, the sun poked through the winter gloom and the thermometer outside the kitchen window hit sixty degrees. I went out to the garage and filled Leverne with gas. Turned the key, pressed the start button. She roared to life. I rode over to my parents' house. My mother rolled her eyes and asked if I was crazy. "Almost was," I told her, "but then I got this bike."

I still have Leverne. Cheap peace. When troubles mount, I climb on and head east down Route 40 all the way to Knightstown. The Greensboro Pike runs north, a twisting road past Civil War homes and stony streams. I roll into Greensboro, past the Quaker cemetery. In the autumn of 1828, the Quaker meeting in that town split. It got so spiteful, they even divided the graveyard. I pull over and walk among the tombstones. Fathers on one side, sons on the other. A sad breach. Maybe if they'd spent more time on motorcycles and less time arguing theology, this falling-out wouldn't have happened. But the first motorcycle wasn't invented until 1885. Fifty-seven years too late to help the Greensboro Quakers.

I'm grateful Leverne the therapist advised occasional frivolity. I hadn't had recess since seventh grade, so I was ready to play. I got to Leverne just in time to keep my spirit from crusting over.

Life is serious, but it can't be taken seriously. At least not always. This tendency to take things seriously likely arises from our need to be in control. That's a burden I'm trying to shake. From now on, I'm letting God head things up. And I'm spending more time on my motorcycle and less time on theology, lest I end up on one side of the graveyard with my sons on the other.

In addition to writing, Philip Gulley
enjoys a ministry of speaking.
If you would like more information,
please contact:

Mr. David Leonards
3612 North Washington Boulevard
Indianapolis, Indiana 46205-3592
(317)926-7566
intleb@prodigy.com